4/05

Songs for a Christian Wedding

ISBN 0-634-05480-5

HAL•LEONARD®
CORPORATION

7777 W. BLUEMOUND RD. P.O. BOX 13819 MILWAUKEE, WI 53213

Visit Hal Leonard Online at
www.halleonard.com

Contents

4   *Answered Prayer*

12   *Celebrate You*

18   *Commitment Song*

22   *Doubly Good to You*

26   *Entreat Me Not to Leave Thee*

40   *Faithful Friend*

33   *Go There with You*

50   *God Causes All Things to Grow*

54   *Household of Faith*

57   *How Beautiful*

66   *I Call It Love*

72   *I Will Be Here*

78   *I Will Never Go*

84   *If You Could See What I See*

91   *In This Very Room*

96   *Jesu, Joy of Man's Desiring*

101   *Listen to Our Hearts*

106   *The Lord's Prayer*

110   *Love*

118   *Love That Will Not Let Me Go*

130   *Love Will Be Our Home*

138   *My Place Is with You*

144   *Ode to Joy*

146   *Panis Angelicus (O Lord Most Holy)*

125   *Parent's Prayer (Let Go of Two)*

150   *Seekers of Your Heart*

154   *Sheep May Safely Graze*

158   *Shine on Us*

163   *Standing in the Son*

170   *This Flame*

182   *'Til the End of Time*

177   *To Keep Love Alive*

188   *The Wedding*

198   *Wedding Prayer*

192   *Where There Is Love*

ANSWERED PRAYER

Words and Music by MIKE JONES
and ANTHONY LITTLE

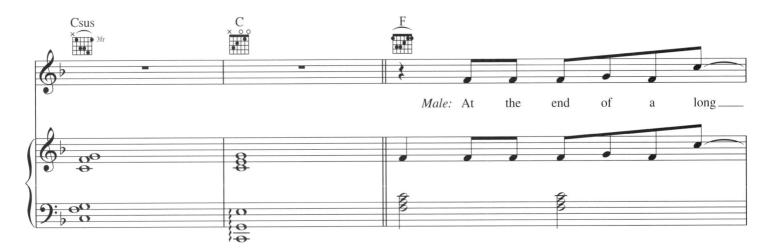

Male: At the end of a long

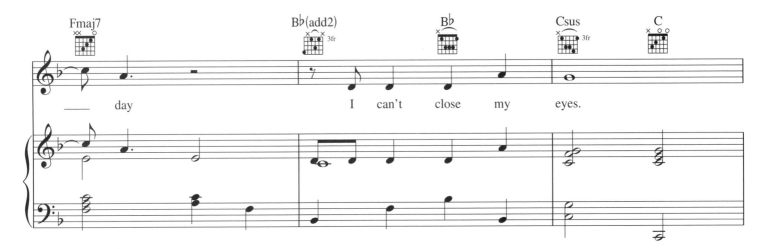

day

I can't close my eyes.

Female: Watch-ing you as the sun _____ sets, as it slow-ly waves _____ good-bye, _____

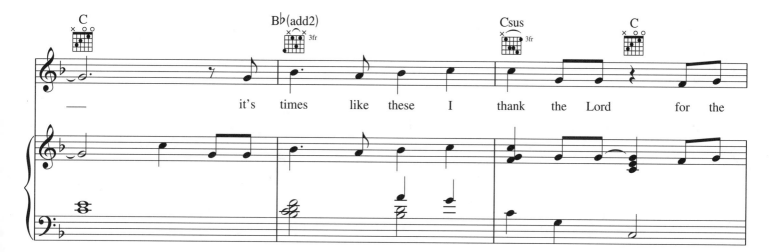

_____ it's times like these I thank the Lord for the

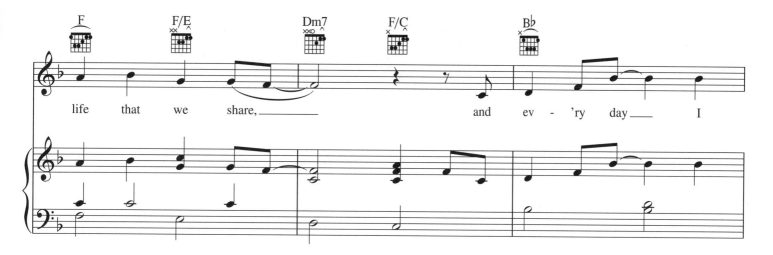

life that we share, _____ and ev-'ry day _____ I

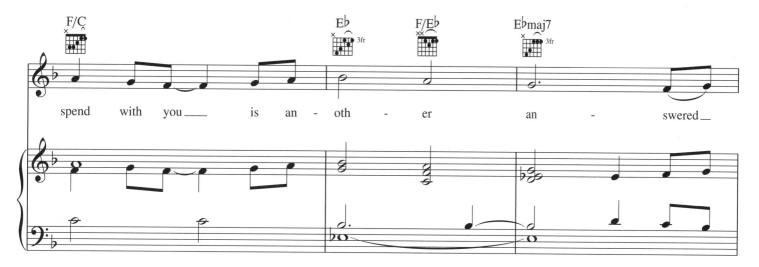

spend with you _____ is an-oth-er an-swered _____

* This phrase is sung both times at written pitch (1st time: high in the male range).
** This phrase is sung both times at written pitch (2nd time: high in the male range).

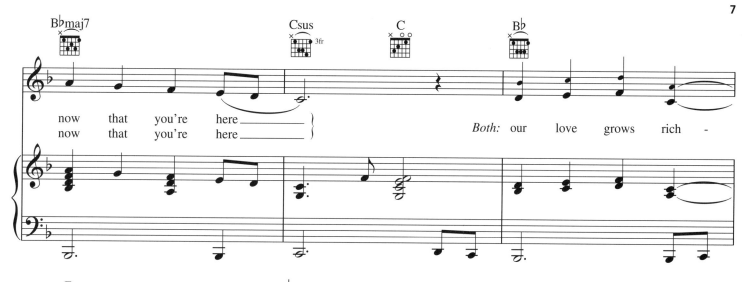

now that you're here _____ } _____ _____ _____ *Both:* our love grows rich -
now that you're here _____ }

- er _____ year af - ter _____ year. _____ *Male:* And if

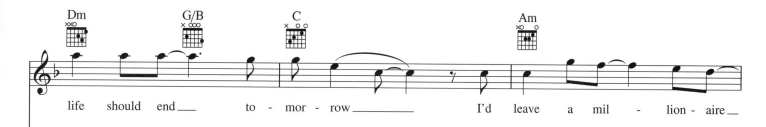

life should end ___ to - mor - row _____ I'd leave a mil - lion - aire ___

_____ *Both:* 'cause in my heart ___ I'd

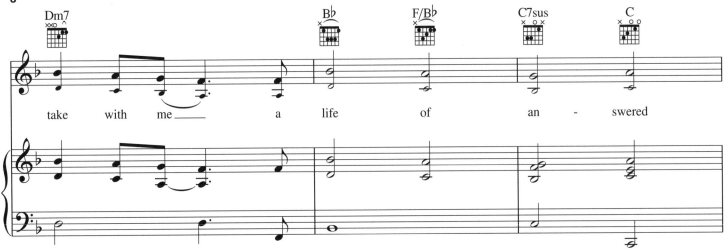

take with me ____ a life of an - swered

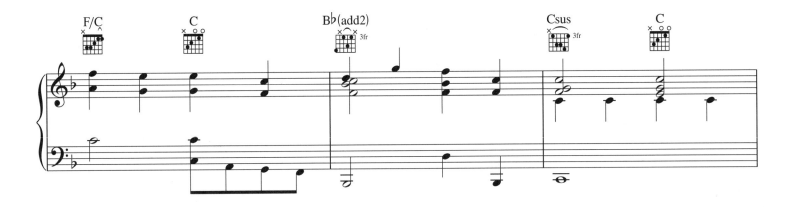

prayer. ____

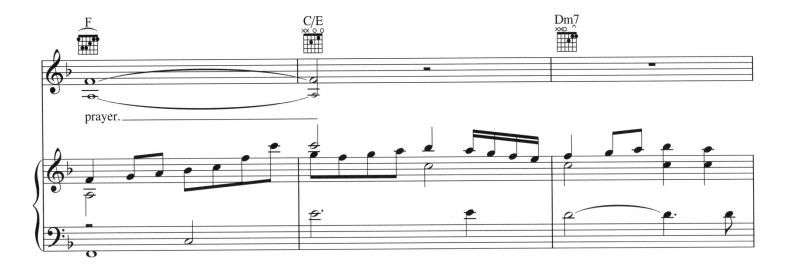

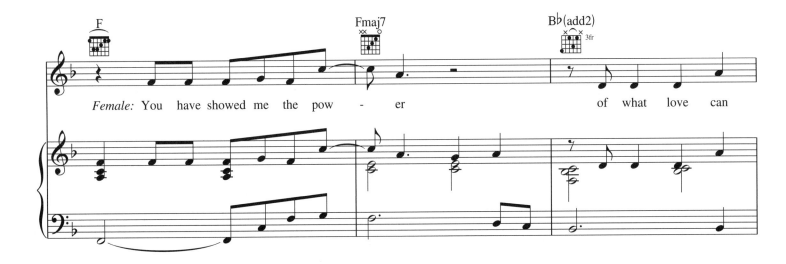

Female: You have showed me the pow - er of what love can

do.

Male: I see glimps - es of heav - en with your

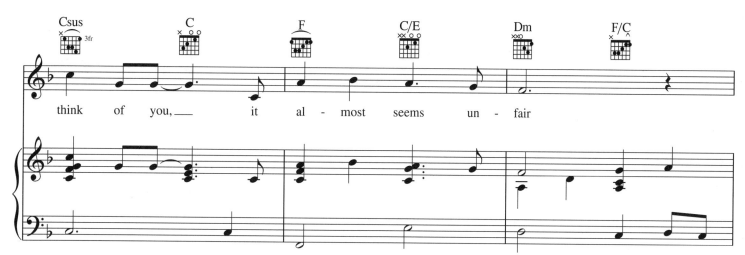

sim - ple "I____ love you." And ev - 'ry time____ I

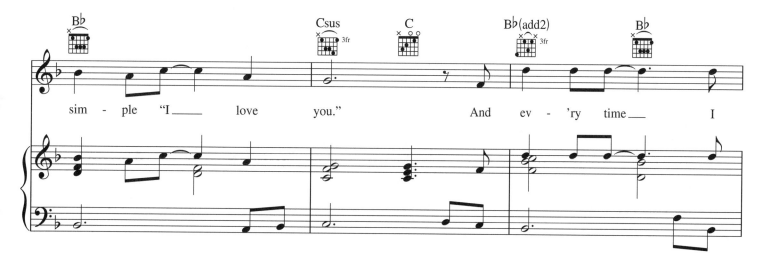

think of you,____ it al - most seems un - fair

for a man____ like me to have so man - y

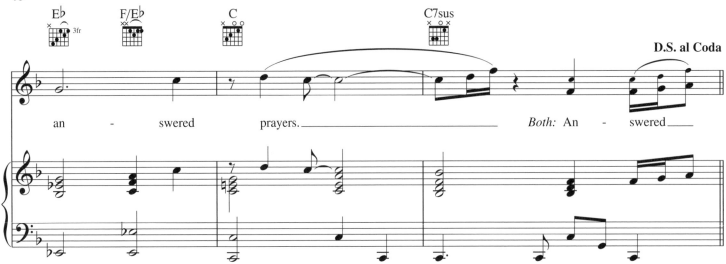

an - swered prayers._____ *Both:* An - swered_____

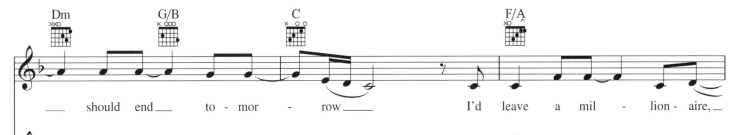

year af - ter ___ year,_____ *Female:* and ___ if life ___
(Year af - ter year.)_____

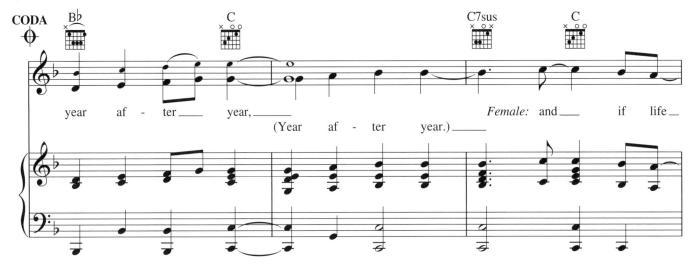

___ should end ___ to - mor - row ___ I'd leave a mil - lion - aire,

Both: 'cause in my heart ___ I'd

CELEBRATE YOU

Words and Music by
STEVEN CURTIS CHAPMAN

Slow, with a beat

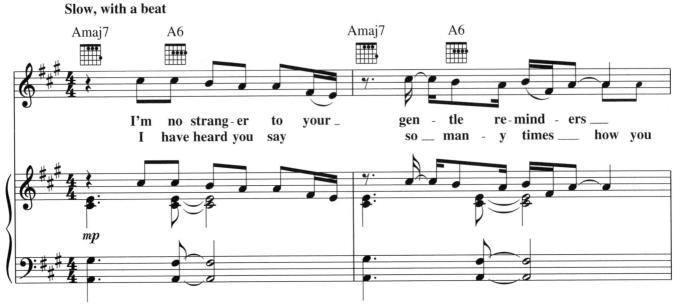

I'm no strang-er to your gen-tle re-mind-ers
I have heard you say so man-y times how you

that the world does not re-volve a-round me.
are sor-ry you're not ev-'ry-thing you should be.

But no soon-er have you spok-en the words, than your
So let me tell you this one more time. There's no

COMMITMENT SONG

Words and Music by ROBERT STERLING
and CHRIS MACHEN

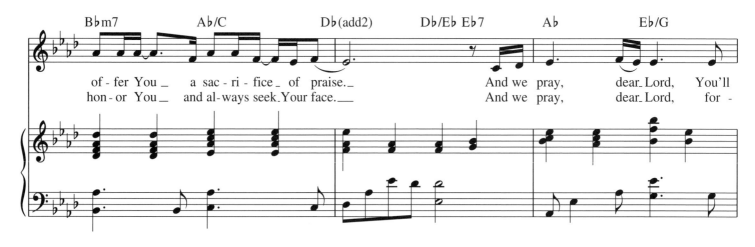

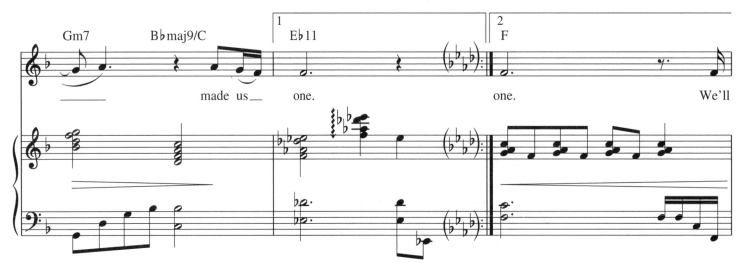

made us___ one.   one.   We'll

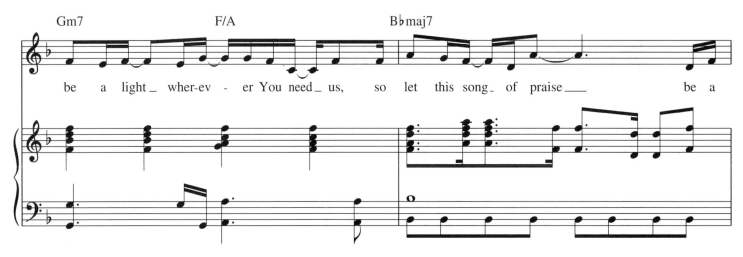

fol - low You _ wher-ev - er You lead _ us,   to - geth-er we'll _ serve You.___   We'll

be a light _ wher-ev - er You need _ us,   so   let   this song _ of praise___   be a

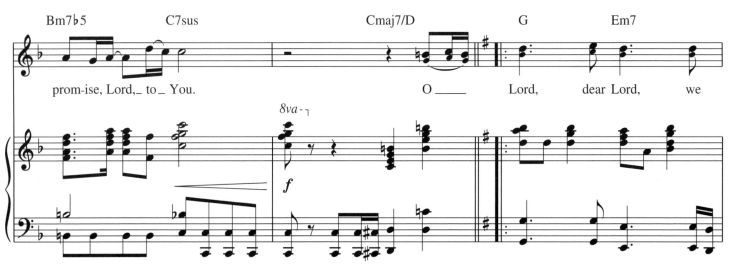

prom-ise, Lord,_ to _ You.   O ___ Lord,   dear Lord,   we

praise Your ho - ly name.__ We're stand-ing here__ to-geth-er to mag-ni-fy__ the Son.__ Let our

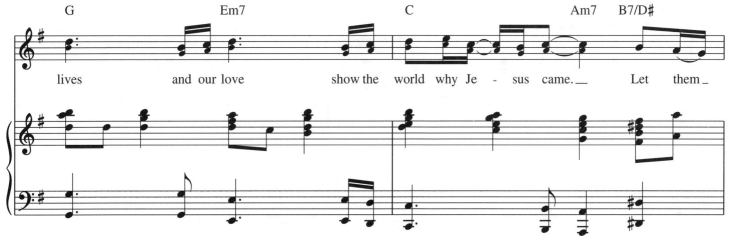

lives and our love show the world why Je - sus came.__ Let them__

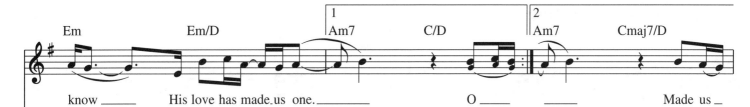

know ____ His love has made__us one._____ O __ ____ Made us __

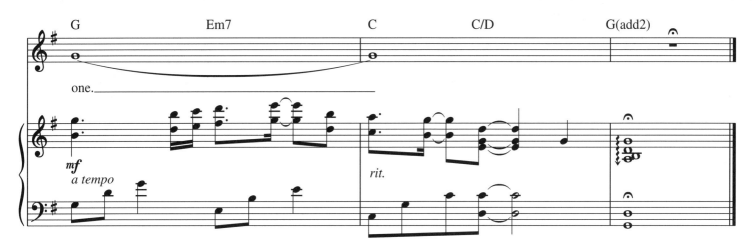

one.__

DOUBLY GOOD TO YOU

Words and Music by
RICHARD MULLINS

If you see the moon ris-ing gent-ly on___ your fields,___
And if you look in the mir-ror at the end of a___ hard___ day,

if the wind blows soft-ly on___ your face,
and you know in your heart___ you have___ not lied.

ENTREAT ME NOT TO LEAVE THEE

Words and Music by
CHARLES GOUNOD

From the Book of Ruth 1:16-17

to re-turn from fol-low-ing af-ter thee, for whith-er thou go-est I will go, and where thou lodg-est I will lodge; whith-er thou go-est I___ will go, and where thou lodg-est___ I will lodge, where thou lodg-est,

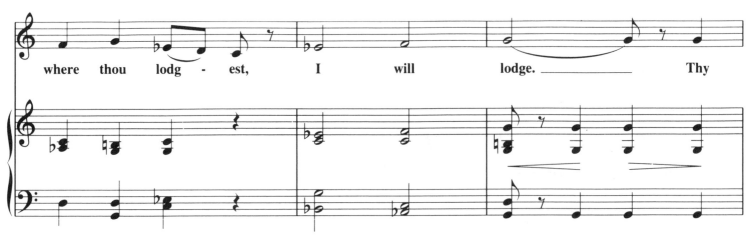

where thou lodg - est, I will lodge. _____ Thy

un poco meno presto, ma pochissimo

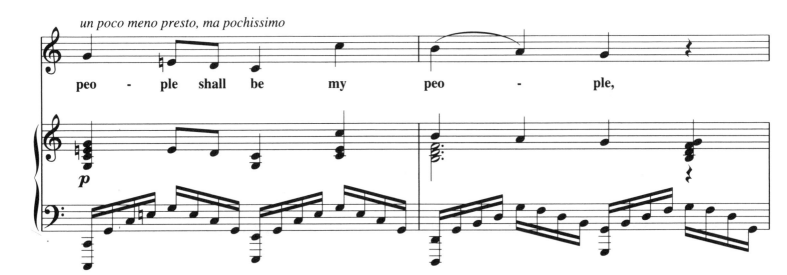

peo - ple shall be my peo - ple,

p

and thy ___ God, my God; _____ thy

peo - ple shall be my peo - ple, and thy

God, _____ my God; _____ Thy

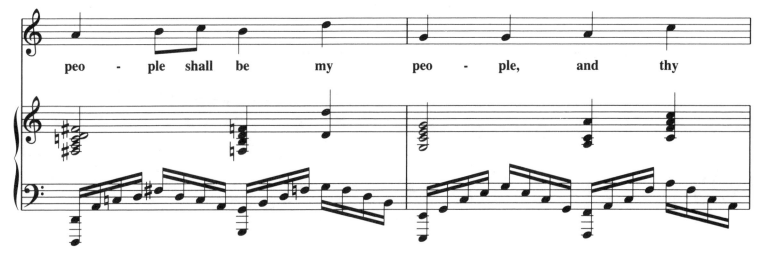

peo - ple shall be my peo - ple, and thy

God, my God. Where thou

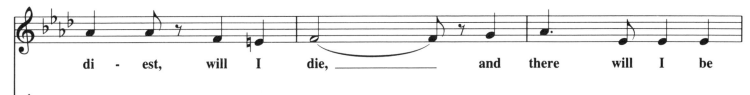

di - est, will I die, _____ and there will I be

bur - ied;___ The Lord do so to me, and more al - so, if aught but

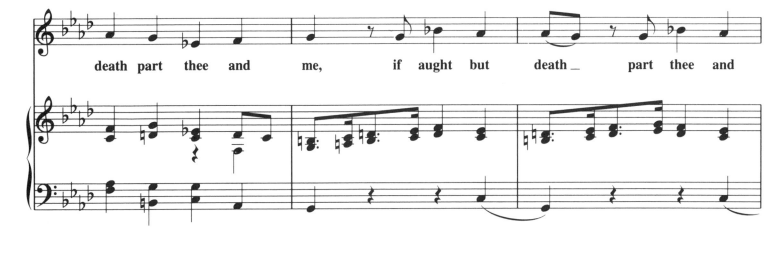

death part thee and me, if aught but death ___ part thee and

me. _____ Thy peo - ple shall be my

peo - ple, and thy ___ God, my

God; _____ Thy peo - ple shall be my

peo - ple, and thy God, _____ my

God; _____ Thy peo - ple shall be my

peo - ple, and thy God, _____ thy

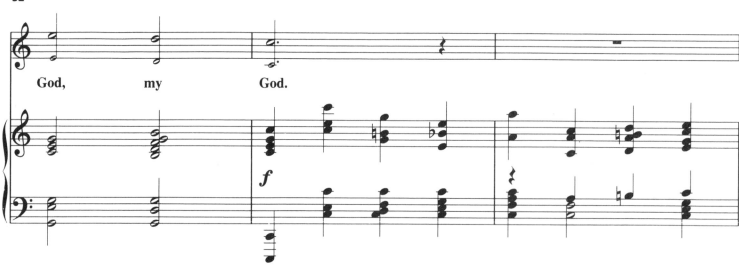

God,   my   God.

GO THERE WITH YOU

Words and Music by
STEVEN CURTIS CHAPMAN

Moderately, with emotion

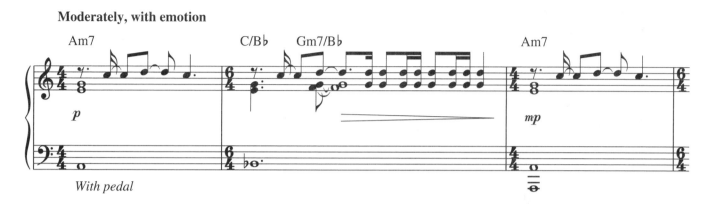

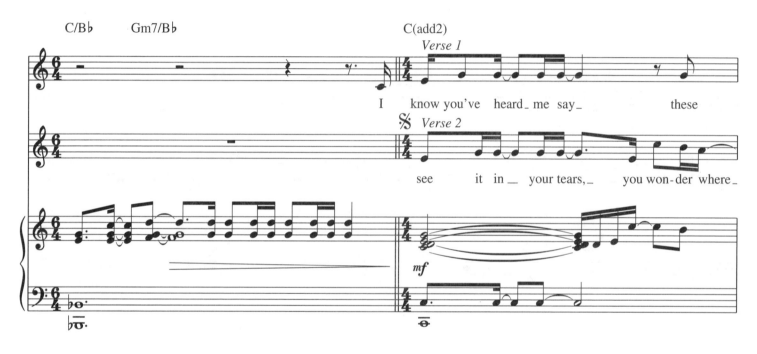

Verse 1

I know you've heard me say these

Verse 2

see it in your tears, you won-der where

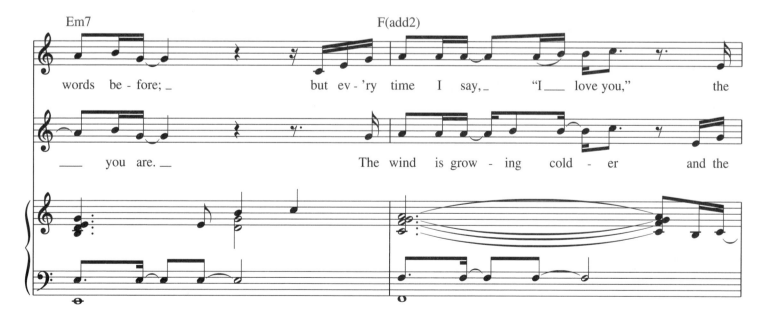

words be-fore; but ev-'ry time I say, "I love you," the

you are. The wind is grow-ing cold-er and the

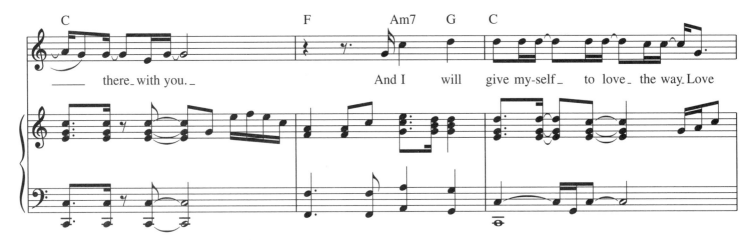

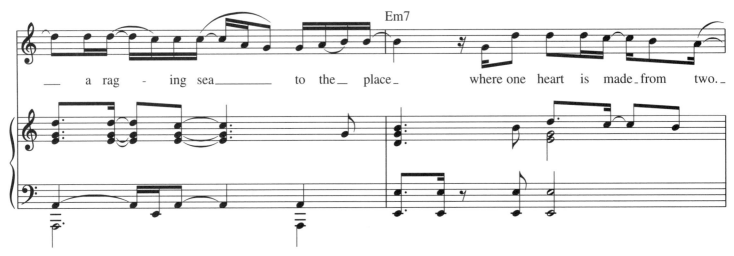

I will go there with you. Oh. I

CODA

there with you. Oh, I know some times I let you down,

but I won't let you go. We'll always be to geth er.

I will take a heart whose na ture is to beat for me a lone and

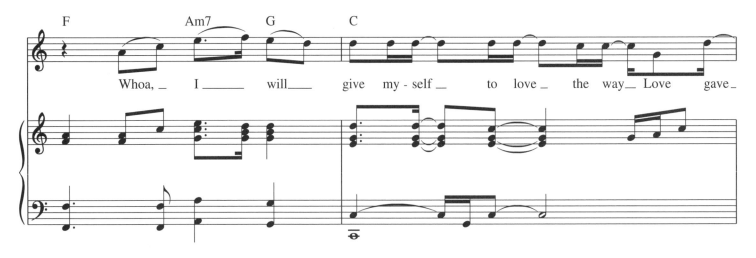

swim a rag - ing sea to the place where one heart is made from two. I will

go there with you. Oh, _____ I will go there with you. Oh, _____ I will

8vb to end (opt.)

go there with you. _____ Oh, _____ I will

go there with you.

FAITHFUL FRIEND

Words and Music by TWILA PARIS
and STEVEN CURTIS CHAPMAN

Quietly

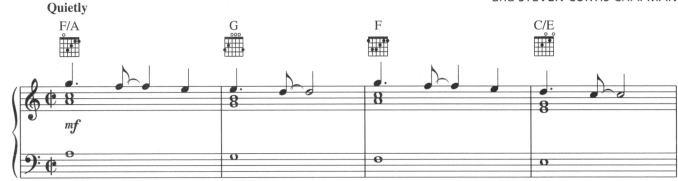

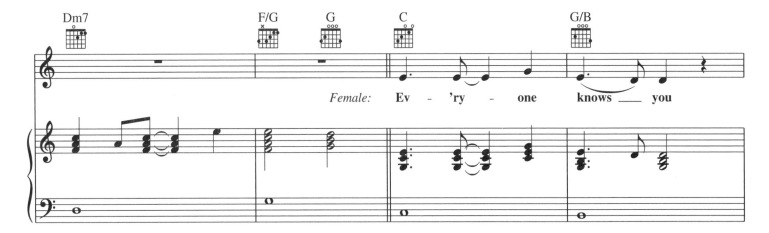

Female: Ev - 'ry - one knows ___ you

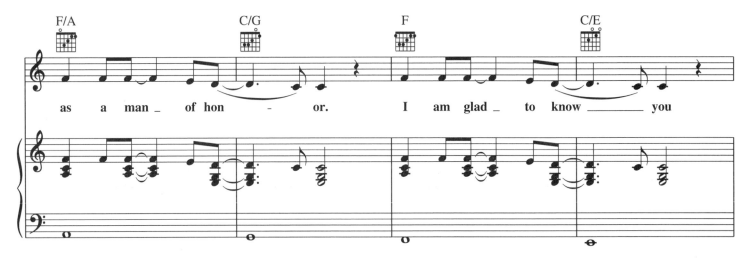

as a man ___ of hon - or. I am glad ___ to know ___ you

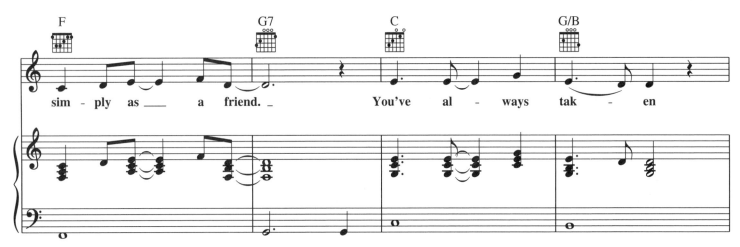

sim - ply as ___ a friend. ___ You've al - ways tak - en

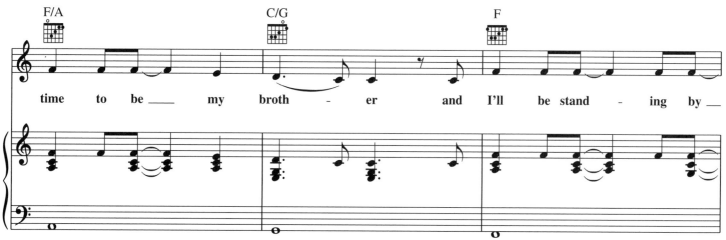

time to be ___ my broth - er and I'll be stand - ing by ___

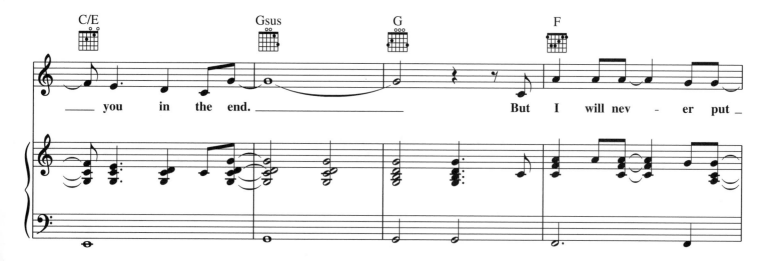

___ you in the end. ___ But I will nev - er put ___

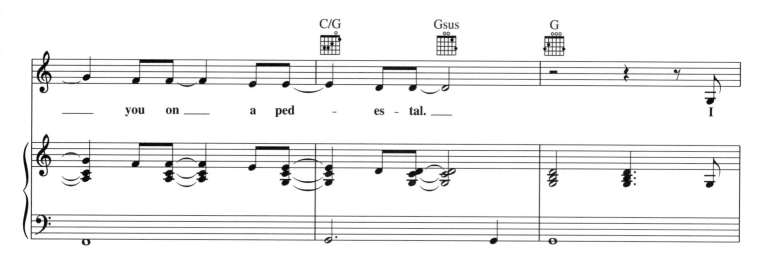

___ you on ___ a ped - es - tal. ___ I

thank the Lord ___ for ev - 'ry - thing ___ you do. ___

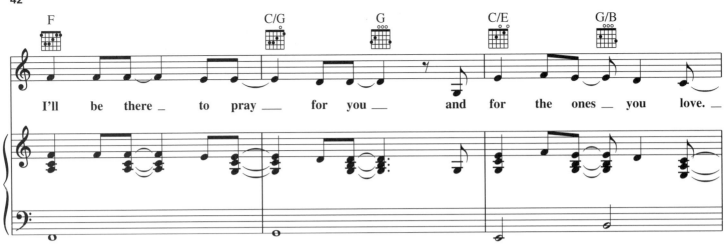

I'll be there _ to pray _ for you _ and for the ones _ you love. _

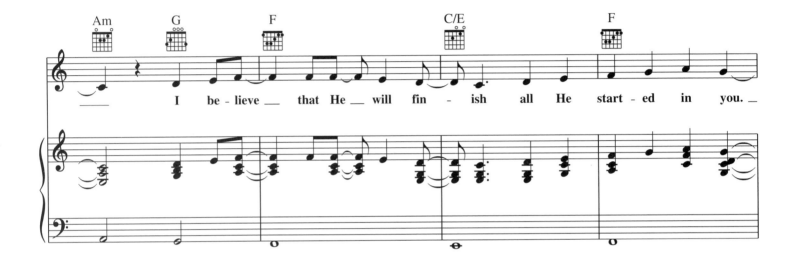

_ I be - lieve _ that He _ will fin - ish all He start - ed in you. _

_ I will be _ an o - pen

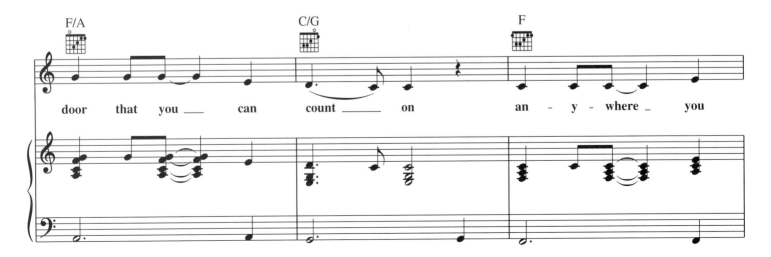

door that you _ can count _ on an - y - where _ you

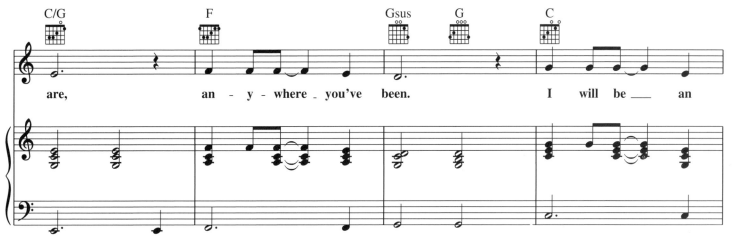

are, an-y-where you've been. I will be __ an

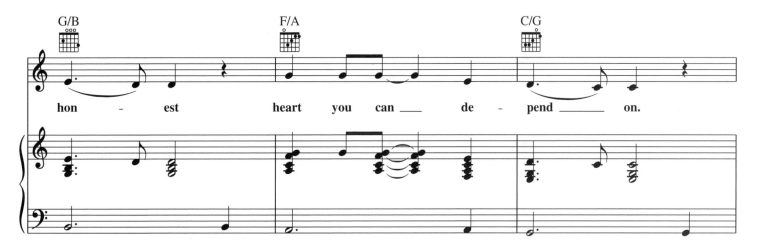

hon - est heart you can __ de - pend _____ on.

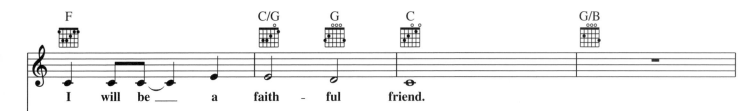

I will be __ a faith - ful friend.

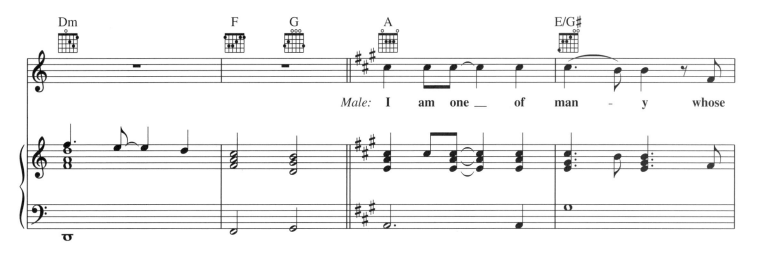

Male: I am one __ of man - y whose

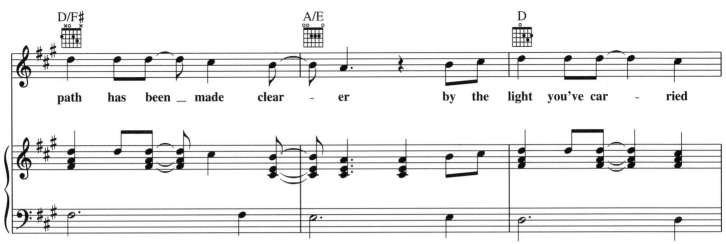

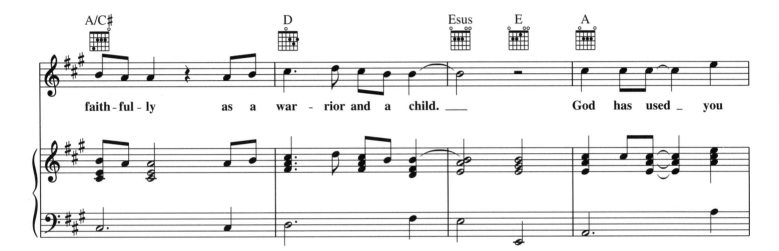

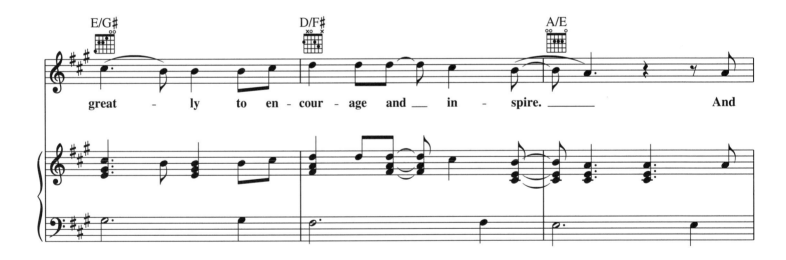

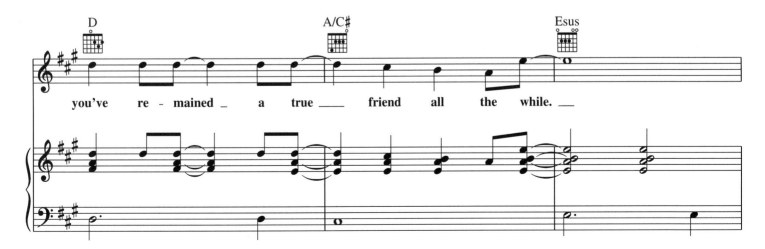

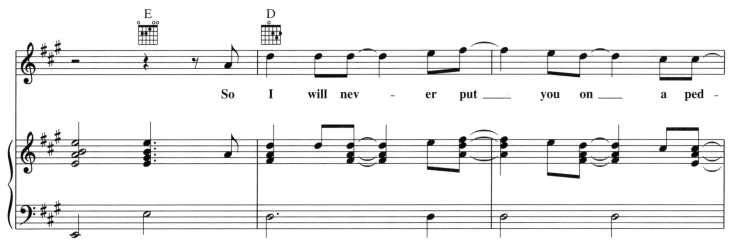

So I will nev - er put ___ you on ___ a ped -

- es - tal ___ 'cause we both know all the glo - ry is the

Lord's. And I'll be there _ to pray _ that He _ will

keep you by _ His grace. _ And I al - ways will _ re - mind _ you to be

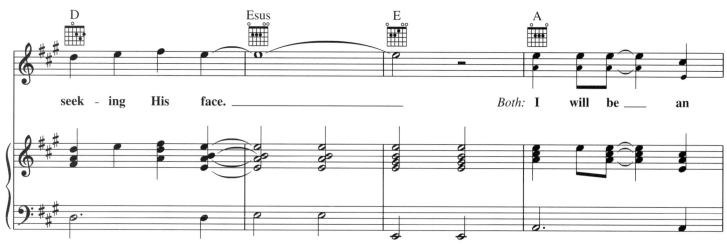

seek - ing His face. _____ *Both:* **I will be ___ an**

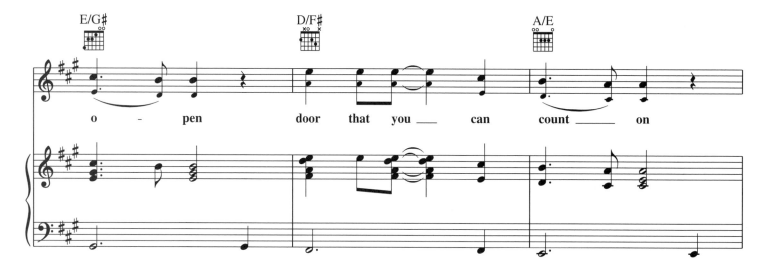

o - pen door that you ___ can count _____ on

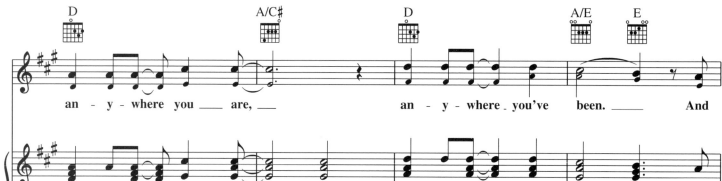

an - y - where you ___ are, ___ an - y - where you've been. _____ And

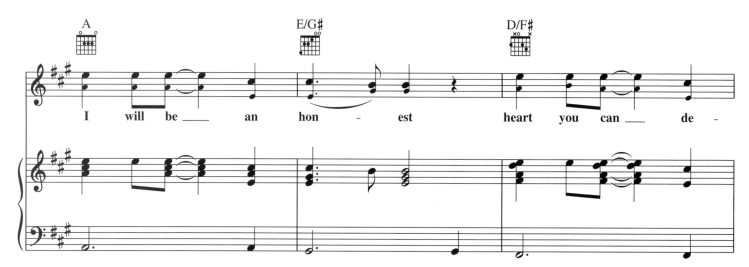

I will be ___ an hon - est heart you can ___ de -

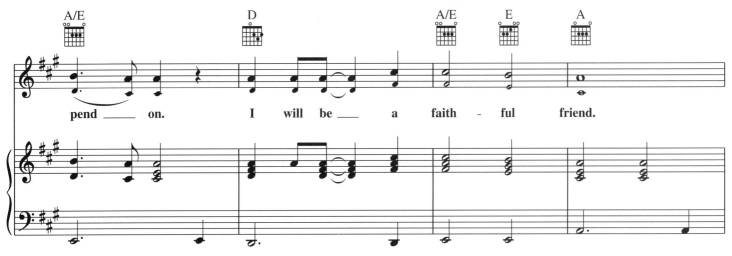

pend ____ on. I will be ____ a faith - ful friend.

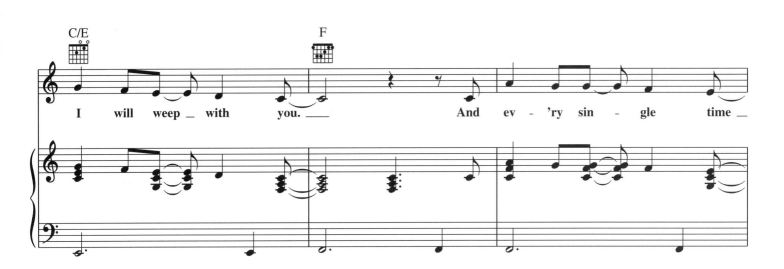

Female: **Should it ev - er come __ your time ____ to mourn, __**

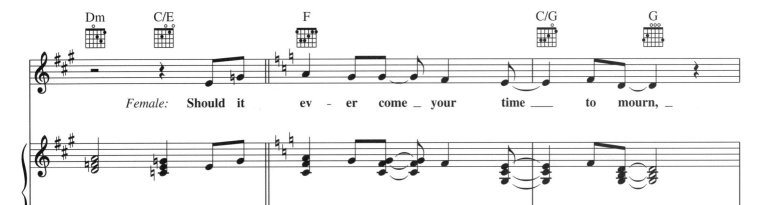

I will weep __ with you. ____ And ev - 'ry sin - gle time __

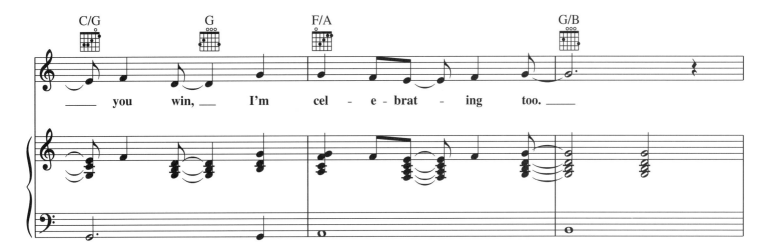

____ you win, __ I'm cel - e - brat - ing too. ____

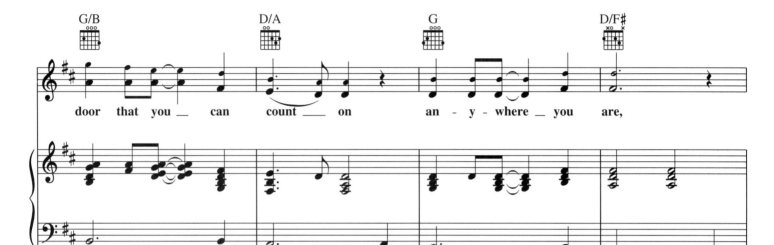

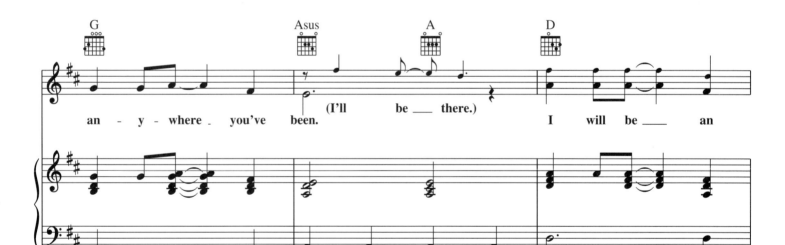

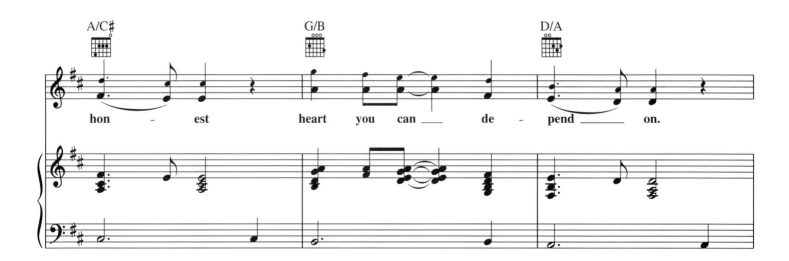

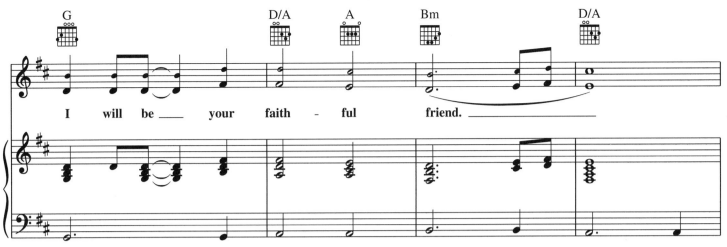

I will be ___ your faith - ful friend. _____

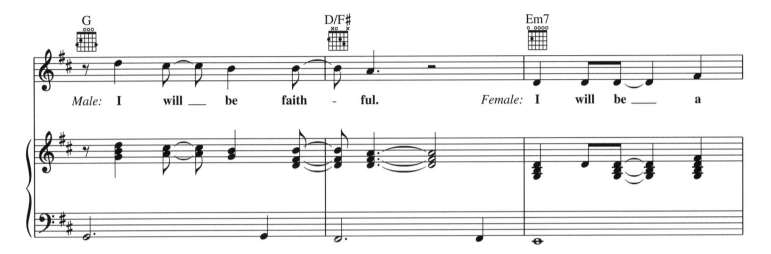

Male: I will ___ be faith - ful. *Female:* I will be ___ a

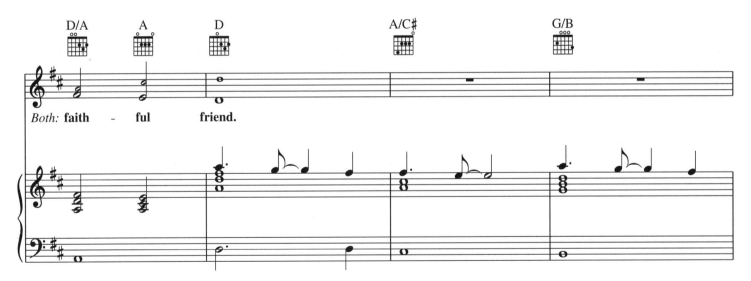

Both: faith - ful friend.

rit.

GOD CAUSES ALL THINGS TO GROW

Words and Music by STEVEN CURTIS CHAPMAN
and STEVE GREEN

With motion (♩ = ca. 96)

Dreams dressed in white,

With pedal

failed; ___ vows made by can-dle-light,
My weak-ness has been ___ un-veiled,

hop-ing to find ___ out what ___ true love is all ___ a-bout. ___
and yet, by grace ___ You choose ___ to love and to ___ for-give. ___

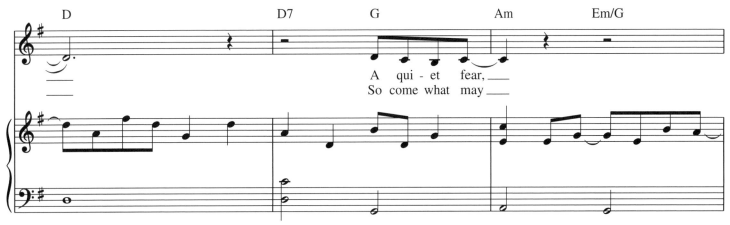

A qui-et fear,___
So come what may___

where do we go ___ from here?
our home is here ___ to stay,

So man-y wake___
a wit-ness to___

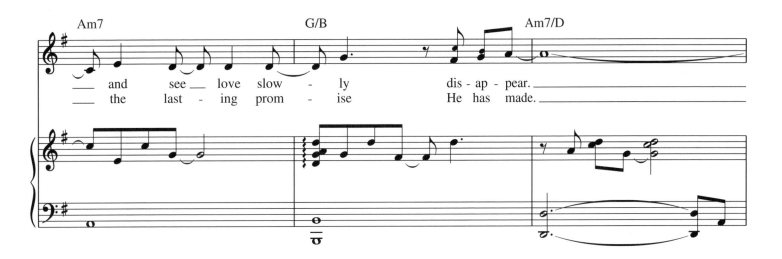

___ and see ___ love slow - ly dis - ap - pear.___
___ the last - ing prom - ise He has made.___

But, God caus - es all ___ things to grow.___

Through ev-'ry sea - son we know_ He will guard_ the life_ that He's

plant - ed in _ our souls._ And when we feel the cold_ winds blow, we'll

hold to what _ we know: God caus - es all things_ to grow._

You know where I've

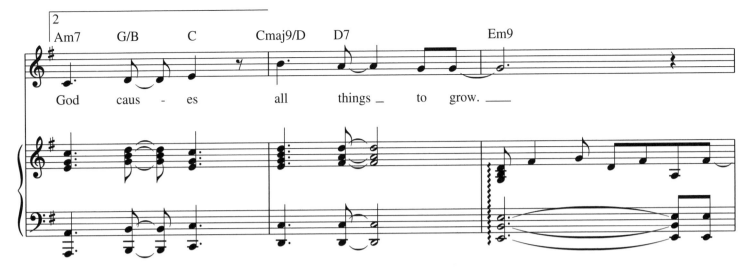

God caus - es all things _ to grow. _

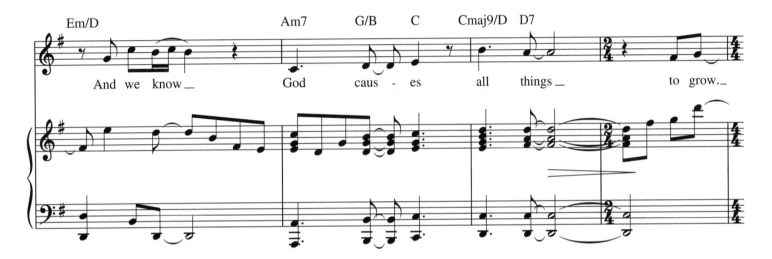

And we know _ God caus - es all things _ to grow. _

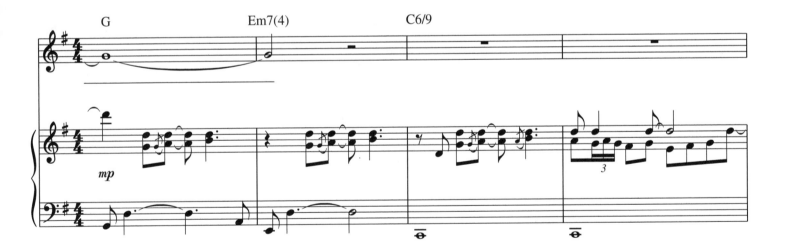

HOUSEHOLD OF FAITH

Words by BRENT LAMB
Music by JOHN ROSASCO

HOW BEAUTIFUL

Words and Music by
TWILA PARIS

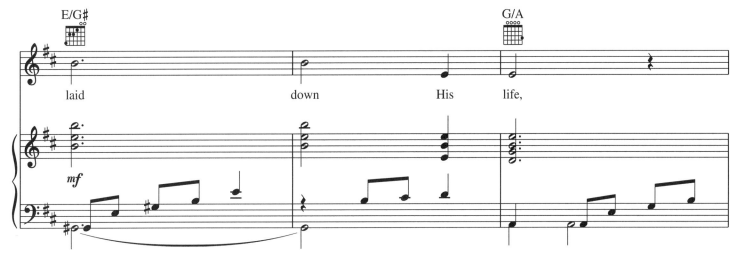

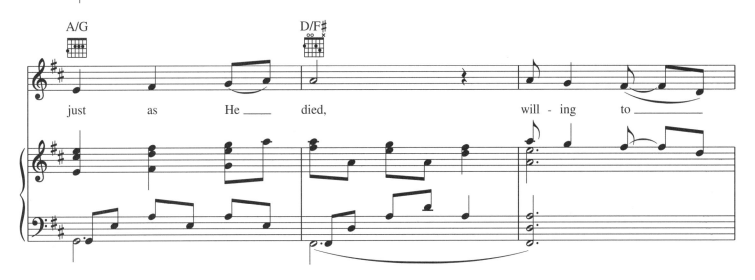

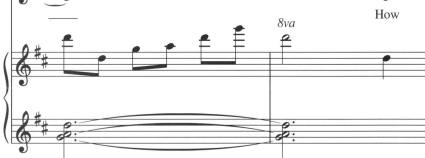

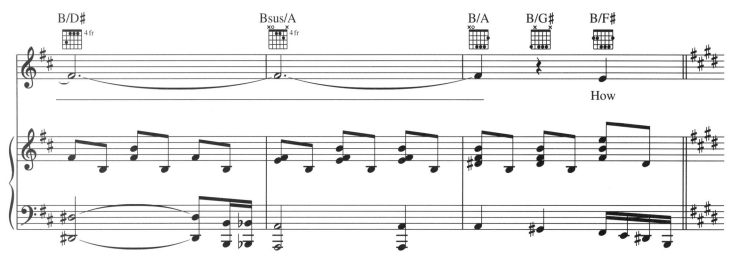

wine and the bread ___ and the sons ___ of the

earth. How ___ beau - ti - ful, ___

___ how ___ beau - ti -

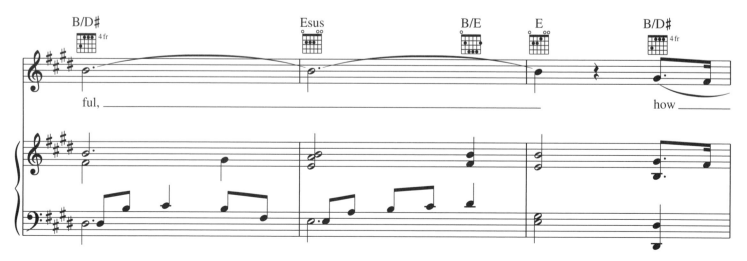

ful, ___ how ___

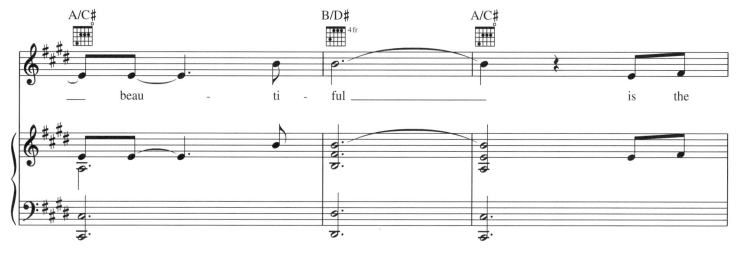

beau - ti - ful _____ is the

bod - y of Christ. _____

rit.

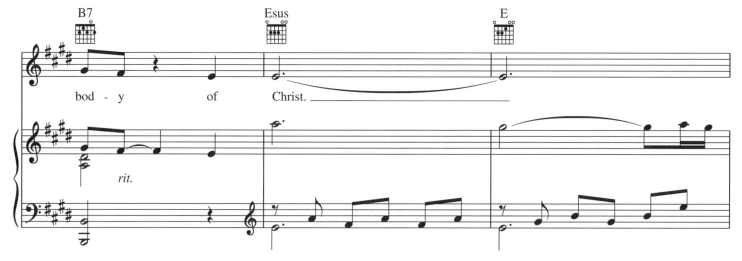

rit.

I CALL IT LOVE

Words and Music by KEITH BROWN
and BILLY SPRAGUE

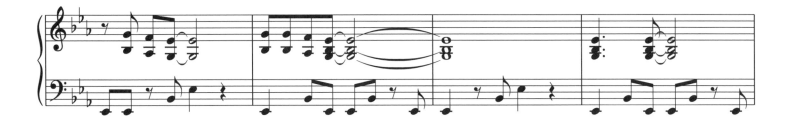

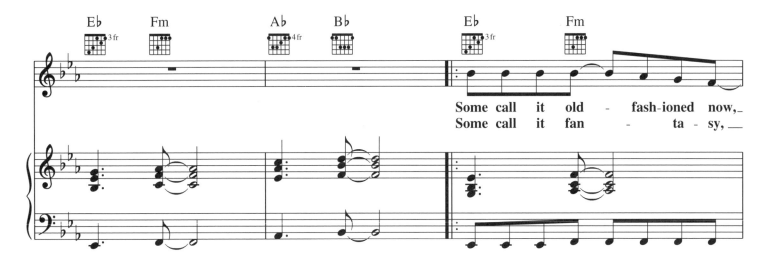

Some call it mak-ing a vow, _____ but I _____ call it
some call it his - to-ry, _____ but I _____ call it

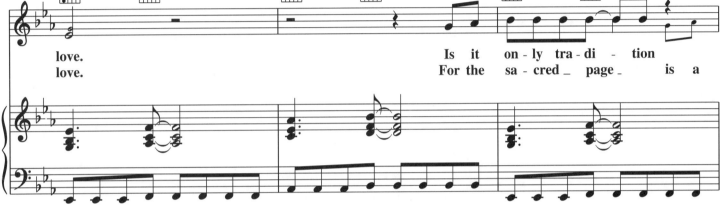

love. Is it on-ly tra-di - tion
love. For the sa-cred_ page _ is a

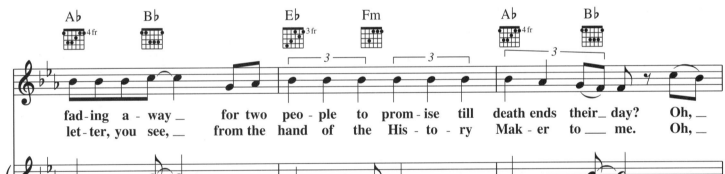

fad-ing a-way _ for two peo-ple to prom-ise till death ends their_ day? Oh, _
let-ter, you see, _ from the hand of the His-to-ry Mak-er to _ me. Oh, _

some call it old - fash-ioned now, but I _____ call it love.
some call it fan - ta-sies, but I _____ call it love.

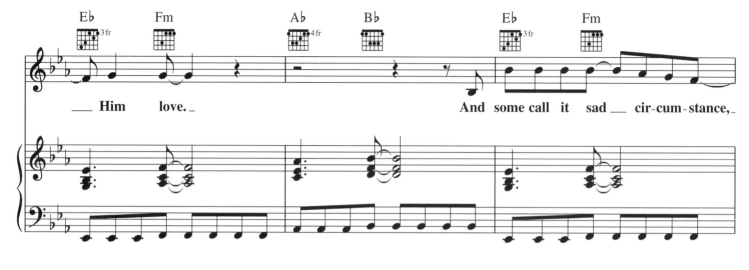

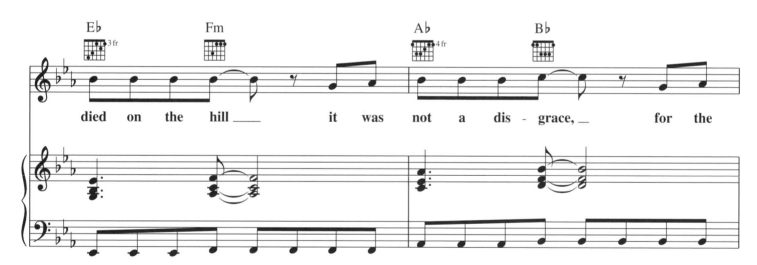

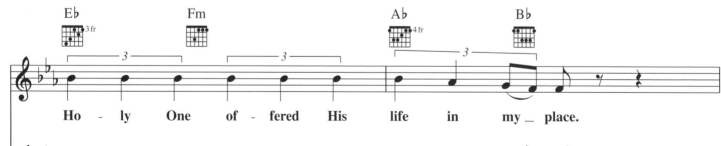

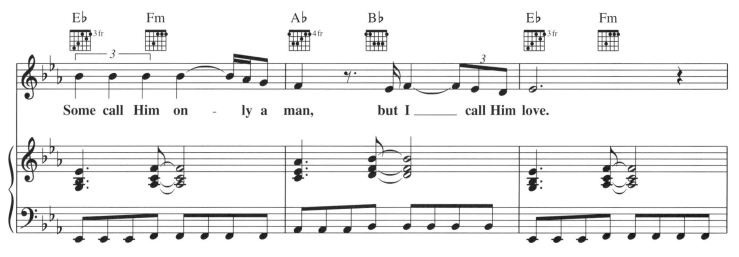

Some call Him on - ly a man, but I _____ call Him love.

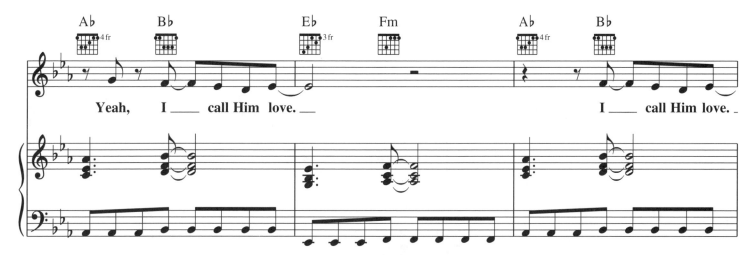

Yeah, I _____ call Him love. _____ I _____ call Him love. _

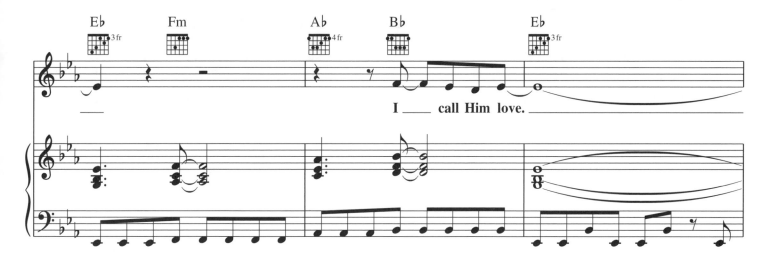

I _____ call Him love. _____

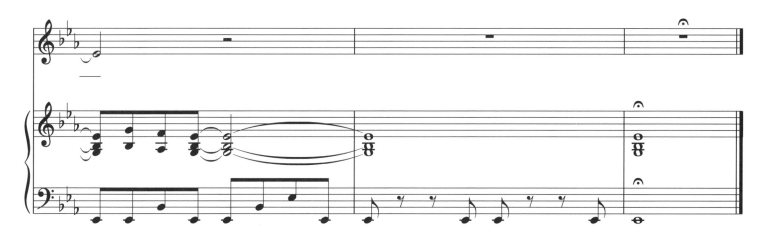

I WILL BE HERE

Words and Music by
STEVEN CURTIS CHAPMAN

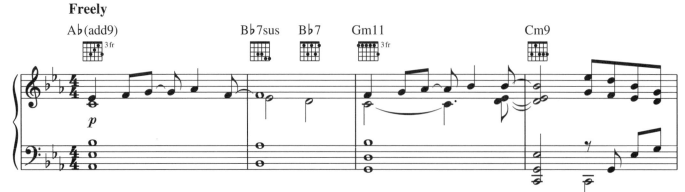

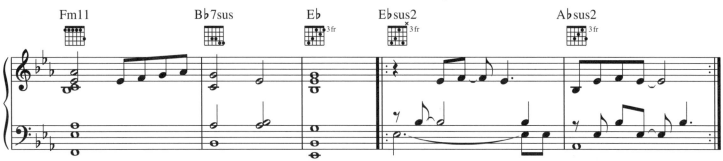

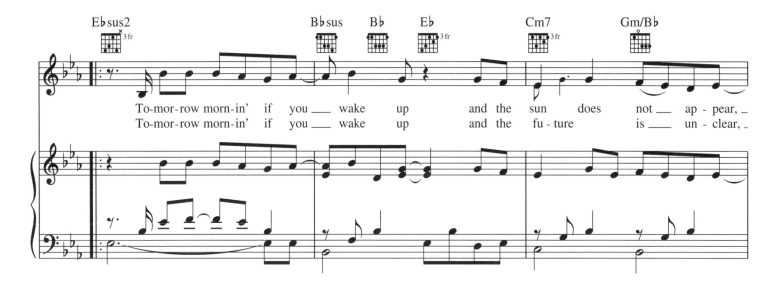

To-mor-row morn-in' if you ___ wake up and the sun does not ___ ap-pear, ___
To-mor-row morn-in' if you ___ wake up and the fu-ture is ___ un-clear, ___

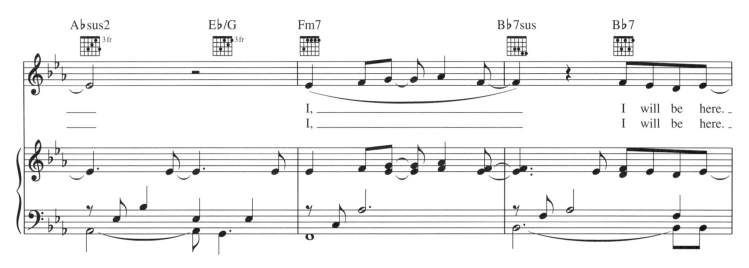

I, _____ I will be here.
I, _____ I will be here.

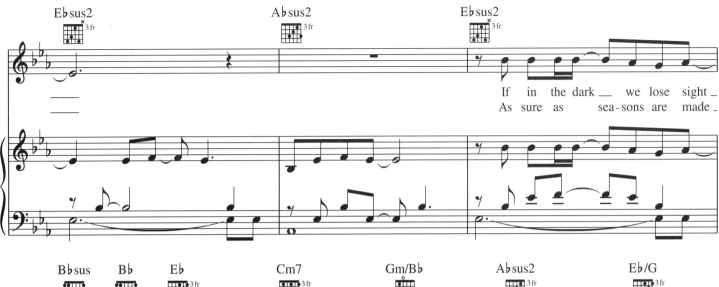

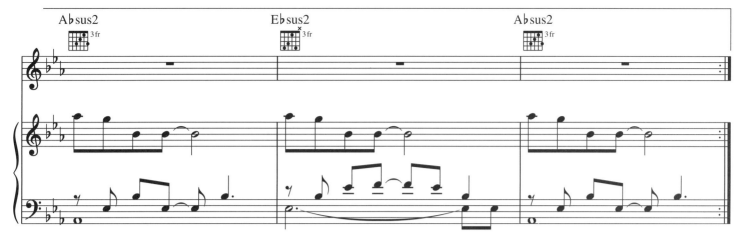

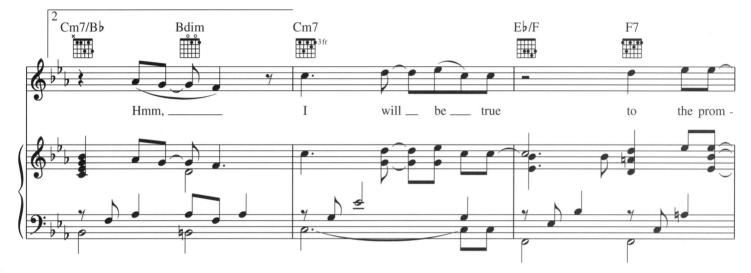

Hmm, _____ I will _ be _ true _____ to the prom -

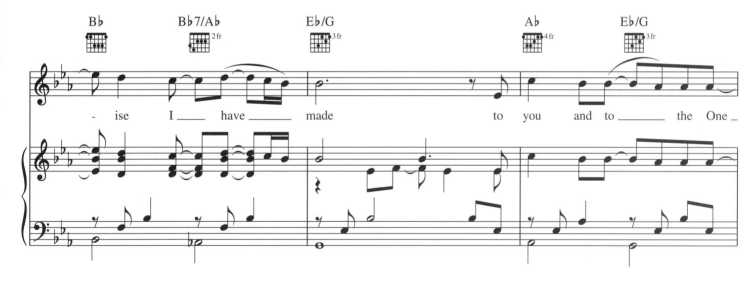

- ise I _ have _____ made _____ to you and to _____ the One _

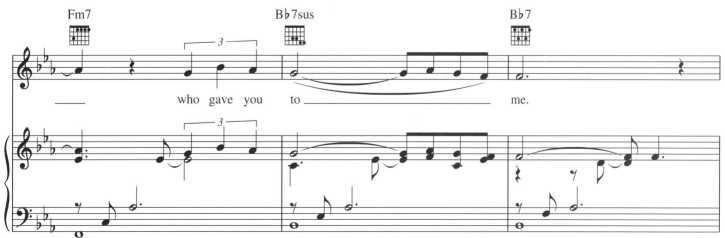

_____ who gave you to _____ me.

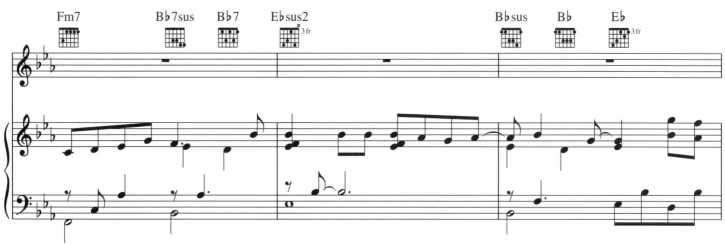

I,

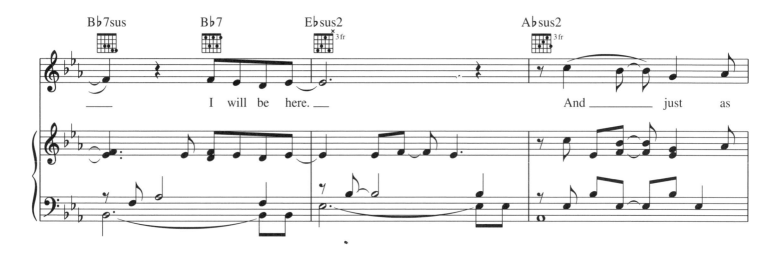

I will be here. And just as

sure as sea-sons are made for change, our life-times are made for

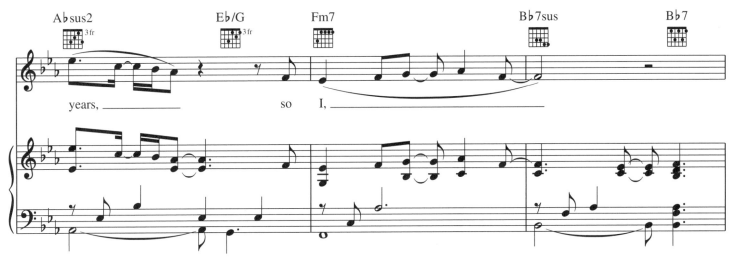

years, _____ so I, _____

I _____ will be _____ here. _____ We'll be to-geth-er. ___

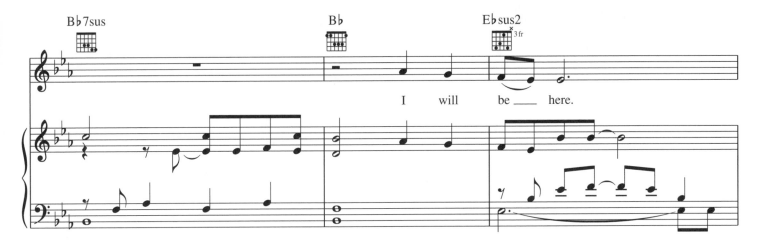

I will be _____ here.

rit.

I WILL NEVER GO

Words and Music by
TWILA PARIS

So man-y peo-ple we know
tears in their eyes
and e-ven
they turn and

more that we don't,
stum-ble a-way,
Have de-
But they can-

IF YOU COULD SEE WHAT I SEE

Words and Music by GEOFF MOORE
and STEVEN CURTIS CHAPMAN

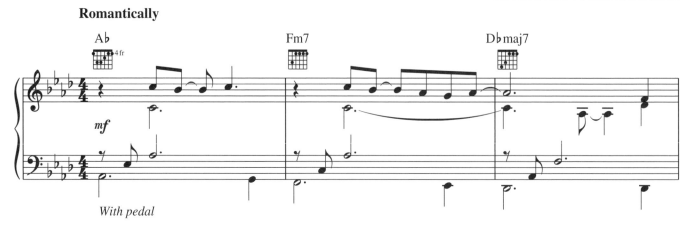

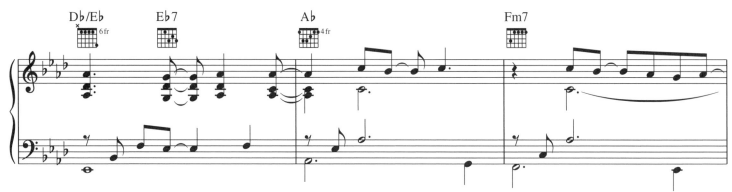

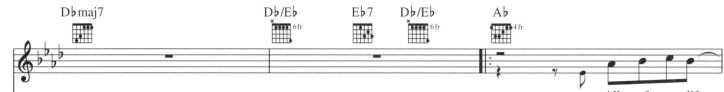

All of my life __
I know there are days __

___ I have dreamed __   that some - how love __ would find me.
___ when you feel _____   so _____ much less __ than i - deal,

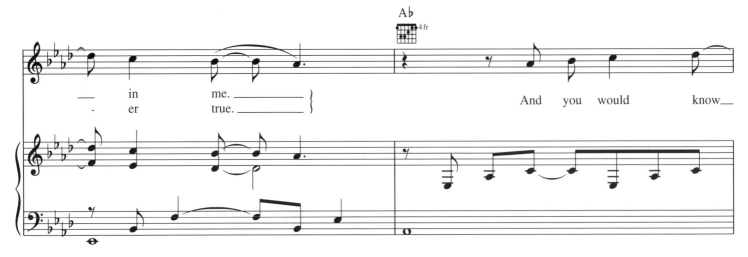

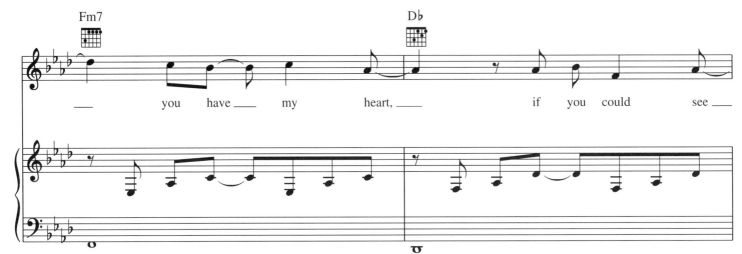

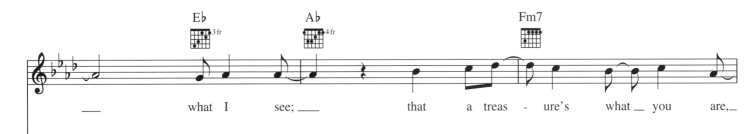

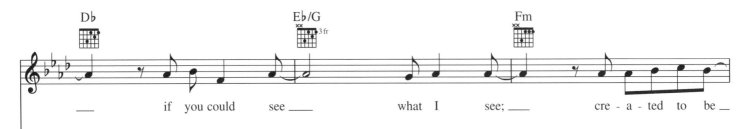

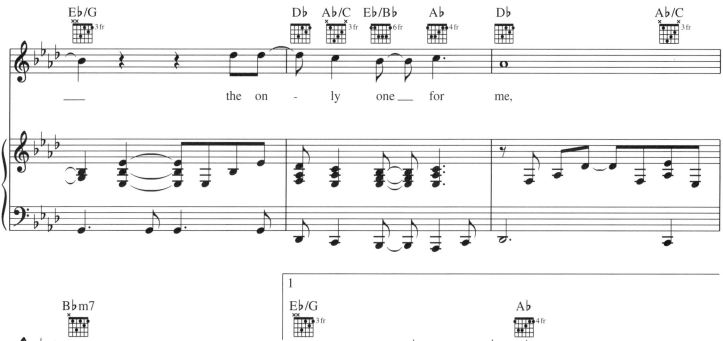

the on - ly one ___ for me,

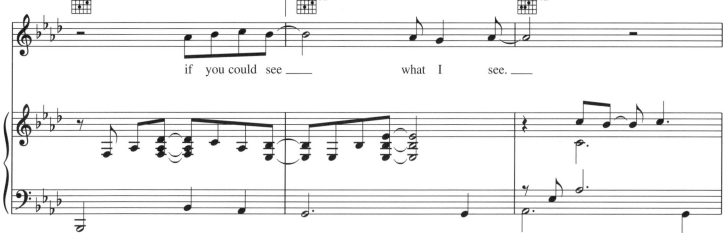

1

if you could see ___ what I see. ___

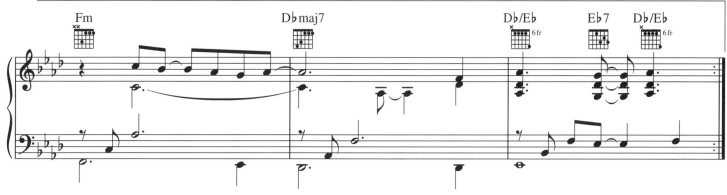

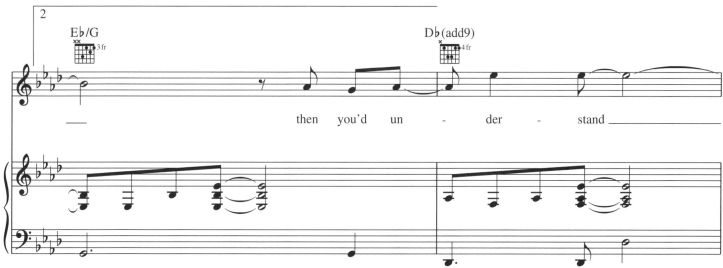

2

then you'd un - der - stand ___

see.

If beau-ty is all ___ in the eye ___

of ___ the be-hold - er, then I ___ am be-hold -

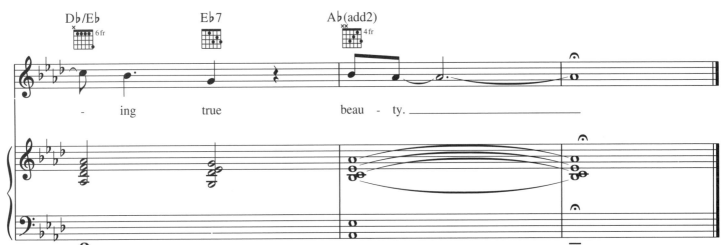

- ing true beau - ty. ___

IN THIS VERY ROOM

Words and Music by
RON and CAROL HARRIS

JESU, JOY OF MAN'S DESIRING

By JOHANN SEBASTIAN BACH

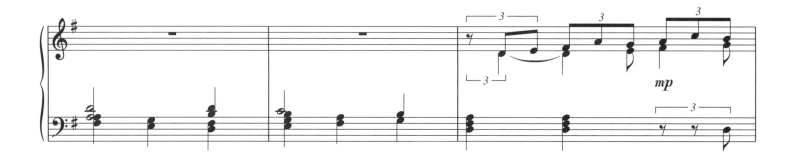

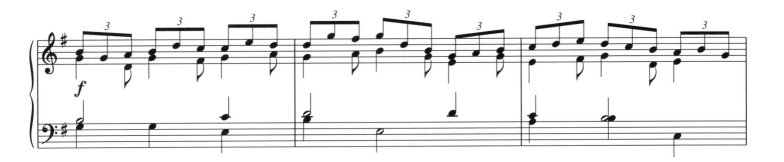

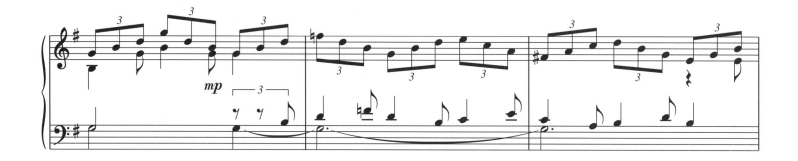

LISTEN TO OUR HEARTS

Words and Music by GEOFF MOORE
and STEVEN CURTIS CHAPMAN

Gentle rhythm

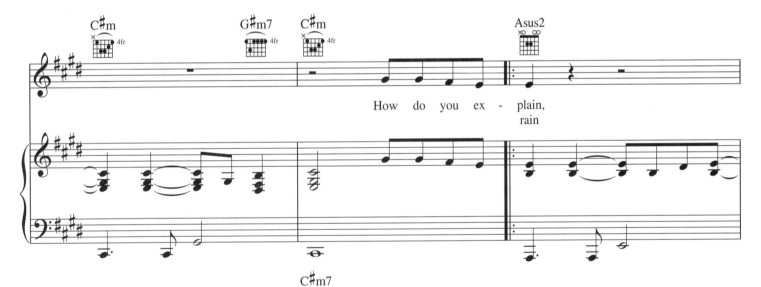

How do you ex - plain,
rain

how do you de - scribe
from these lips of mine,

a love that goes from
and if I had a

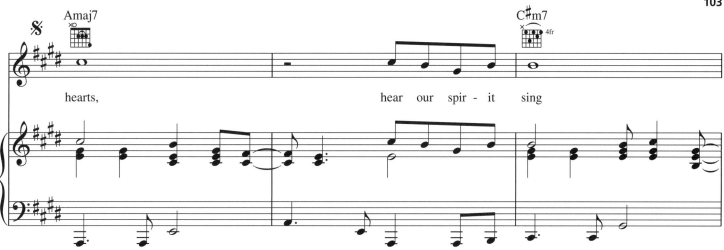

hearts, hear our spir - it sing

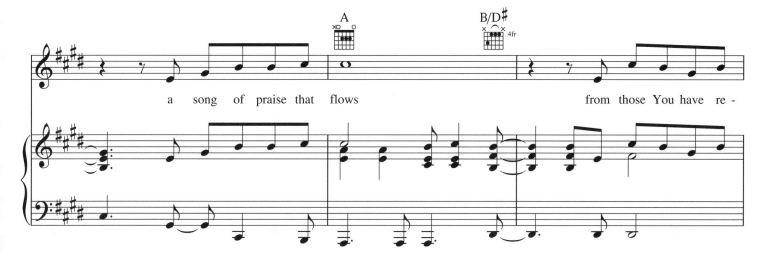

a song of praise that flows from those You have re -

deemed. We will use the words we know to

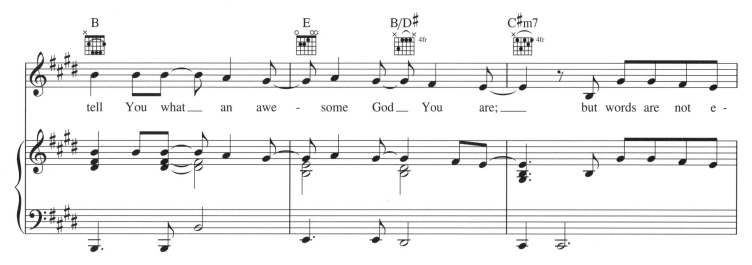

tell You what an awe - some God You are; but words are not e -

To Coda ⊕

nough to tell You of our love, so lis-ten to our hearts.

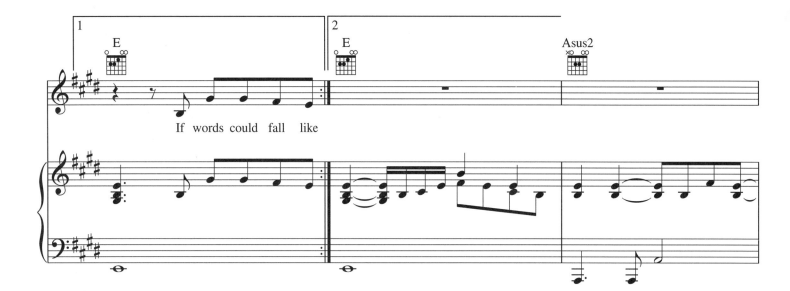

If words could fall like

THE LORD'S PRAYER

By ALBERT H. MALOTTE

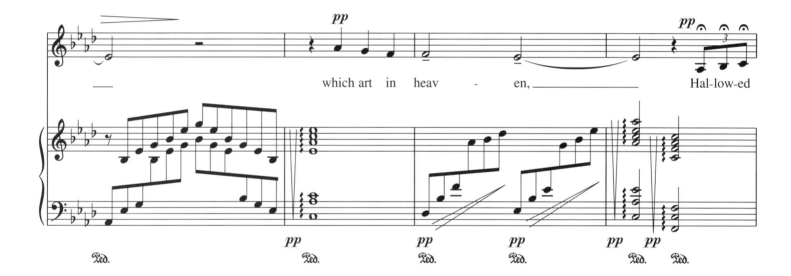

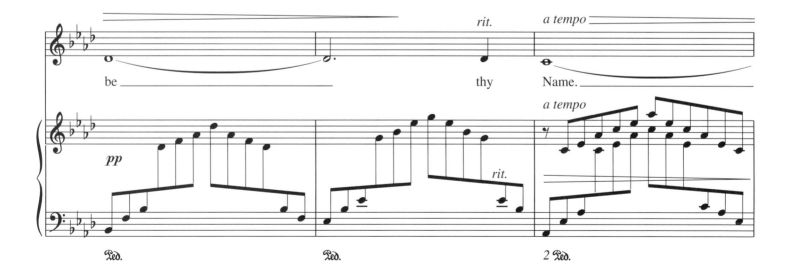

Give us this day our dai - ly bread. And for - give us our debts, _____ As we _____ for-give our debt - ors. And lead us not in - to temp - ta - tion; But de -

LOVE

Words and Music by
BOB HARTMAN

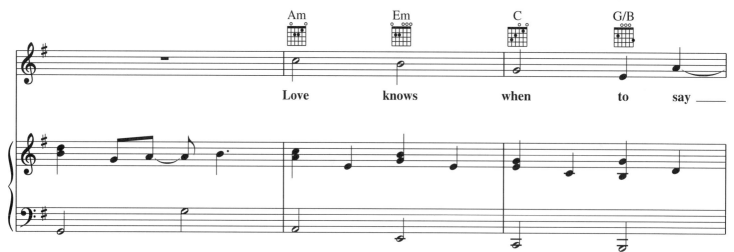

Love knows when to say ___

___ no. Love grows

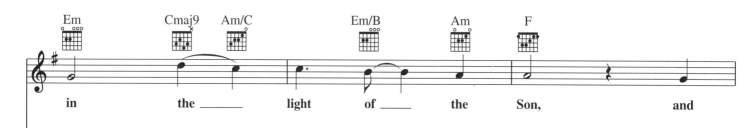

in the ___ light of ___ the Son, and

love shows the world ___ that the Son of ___

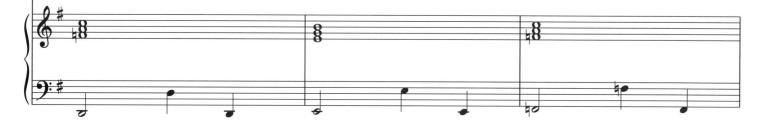

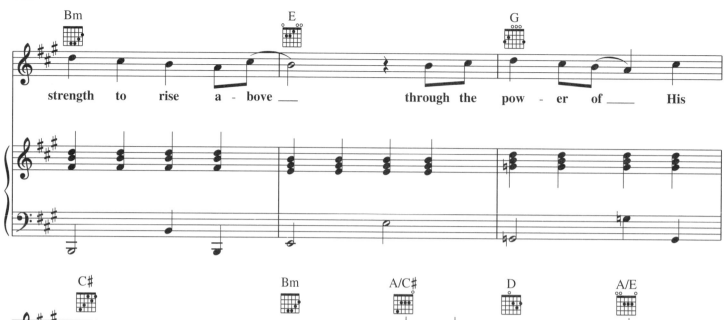

strength to rise a - bove ___ through the pow - er of ___ His

love. Lord, we need to know _ the pow - er of ___ Your

love. ___ Love knows

when to let ___ go. ___ Love knows

when to say ____ no. _____ Love grows

in the ____ light of ___ the Son, and love shows the world ____

____ that the Son of _____ Love has _____ come. _____

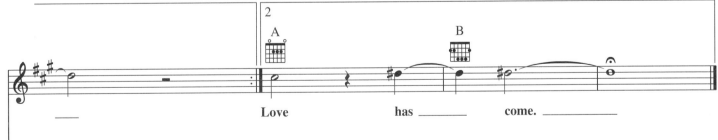

Love has _____ come. _____

LOVE THAT WILL NOT LET ME GO

Words and Music by STEVE CAMP
and ROB FRAZIER

Rubato

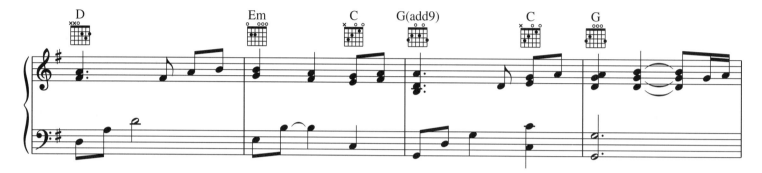

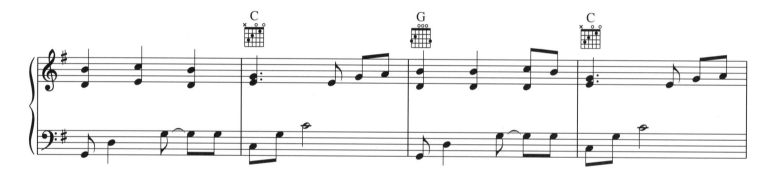

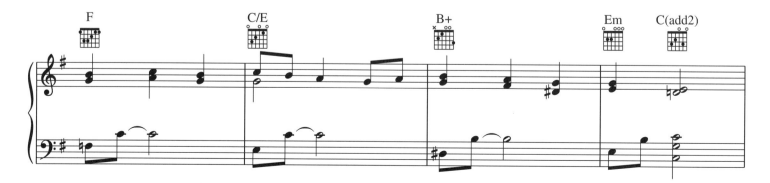

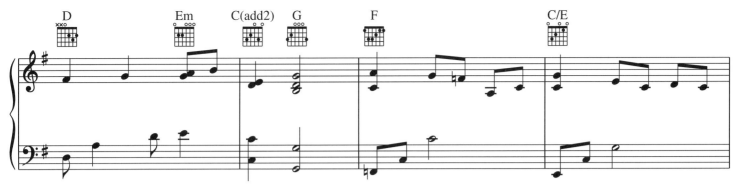

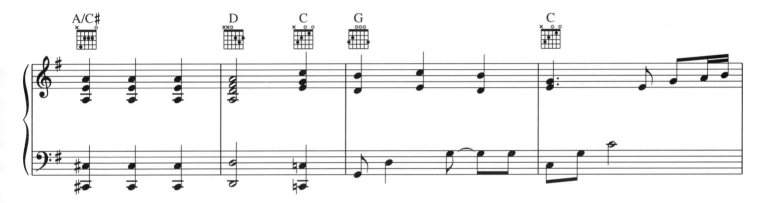

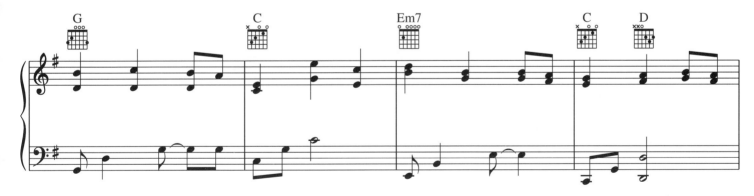

Slowly, in tempo

In this wea - ry world, __ chas - ing af - ter dreams __
Lord, You al - ways knew__ the road that I __ would take, __

__ just led me back where I start - ed. _____
__ then You saved me just in time. ____

I could - n't see __ my way __ to find a hid - ing place __
What I owe __ to You __ I could not __ re - pay, __

__ for the bro - ken - heart - ed.
__ so I pledge __ You my whole life. ____

Rubato

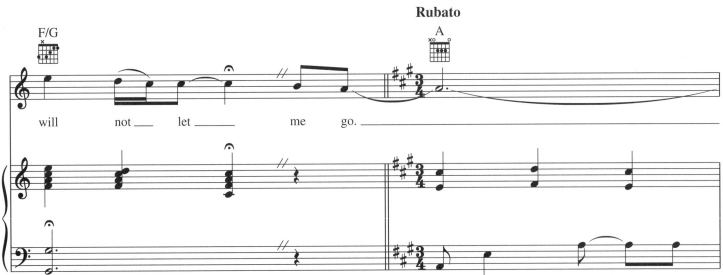

will not ___ let _____ me go. _____

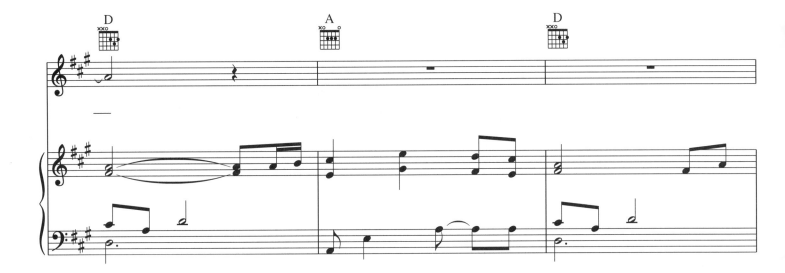

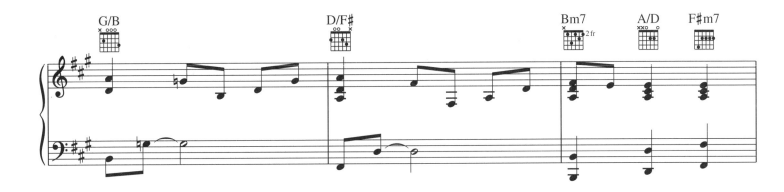

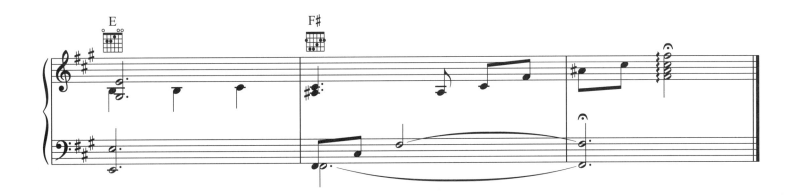

PARENT'S PRAYER
(Let Go of Two)

Words and Music by
GREG DAVIS

With feeling

I guess we have al - ways known _ that a
Now in your ten - der care, _ Lord, _

day like this _ one would come, _
be all that we _ can - not be. _

when our chil - dren would leave _
And help us to trust _

_ us and be - gin to build a home of their own. _
_ You when we don't see You quick - ly meet - ing their needs. _

LOVE WILL BE OUR HOME

Words and Music by
STEVEN CURTIS CHAPMAN

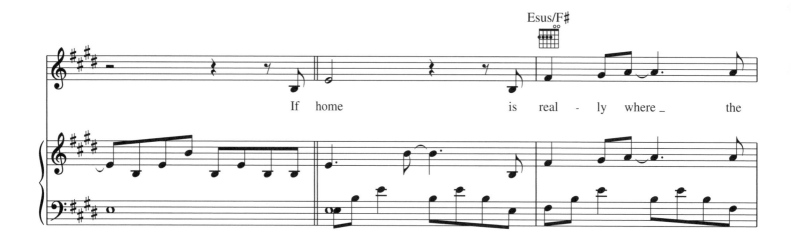

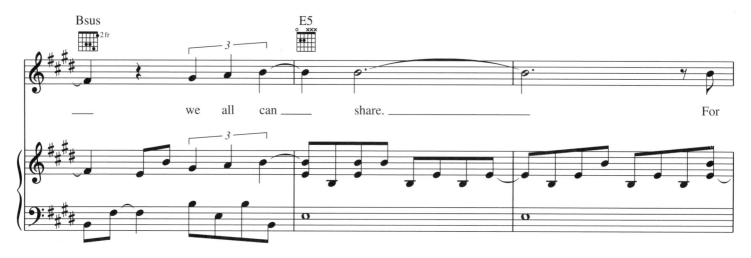

even with our dif-f'ren-ces, our hearts are much the same.

For where love is, we come to-geth-er there.

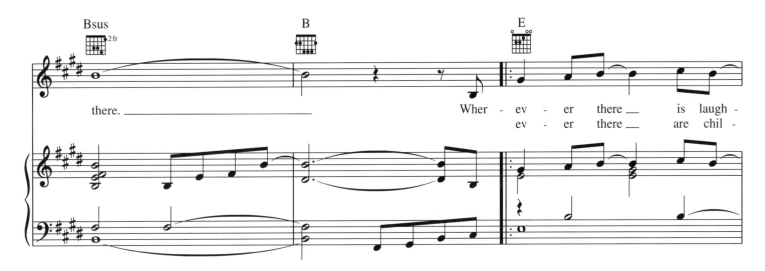

Wher-ev-er there is laugh-
ev-er there are chil-

-ter ring-ing, some-one smil-ing, some-one dream-ing,
-dren sing-ing, where a ten-der heart is beat-ing,

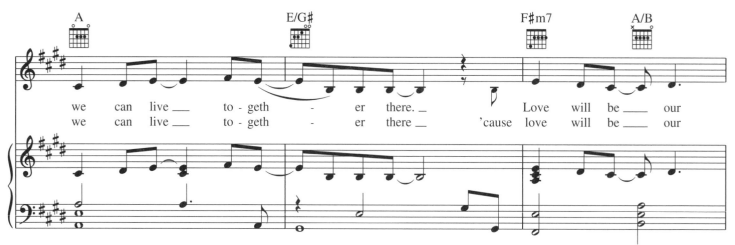

we can live ___ to - geth - er there. ___ Love will be ___ our
we can live ___ to - geth - er there ___ 'cause love will be ___ our

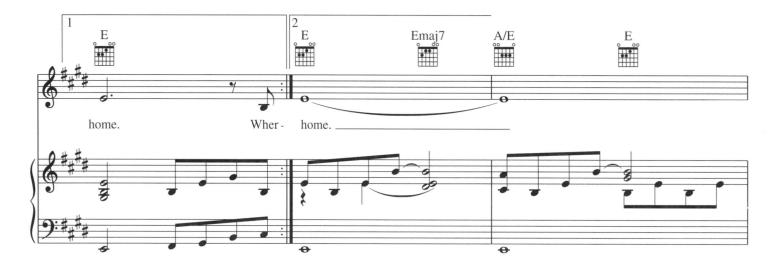

home.
Wher - home. ___

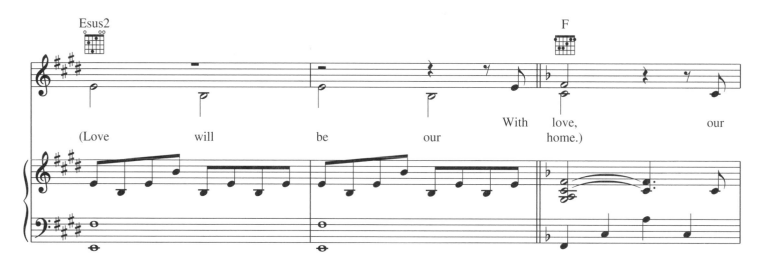

(Love will be our
With love, home.) our

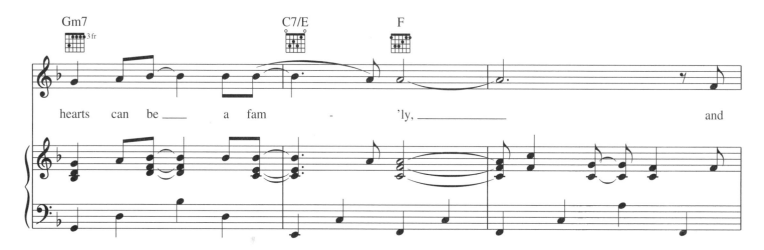

hearts can be ___ a fam - 'ly, ___ and

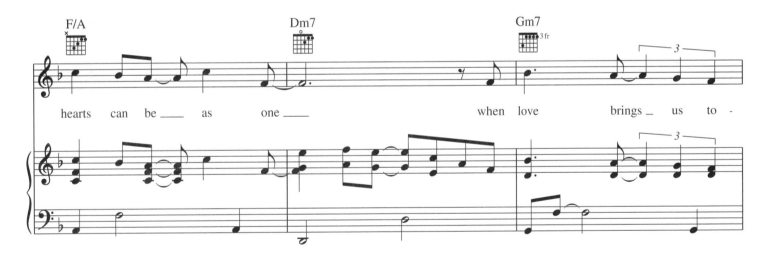

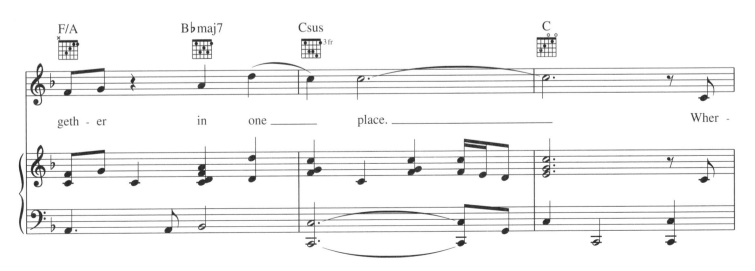

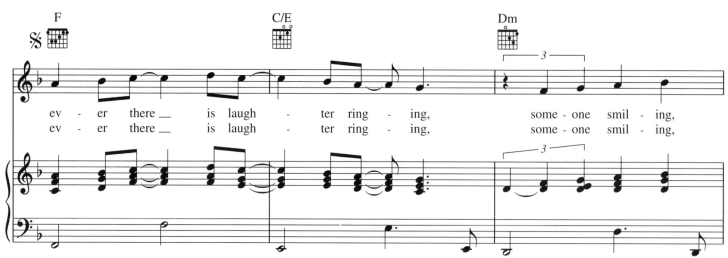

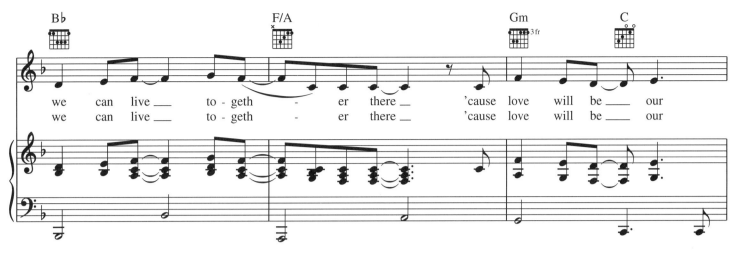

we can live ___ to - geth - er there ___ 'cause love will be ___ our
we can live ___ to - geth - er there ___ 'cause love will be ___ our

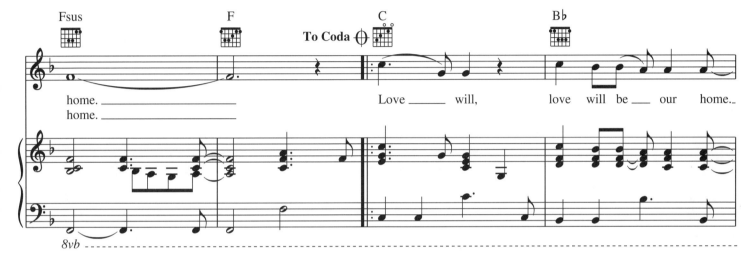

home. ___
home. ___

Love ___ will, love will be ___ our home. ___

Love ___ will, love will be ___ our

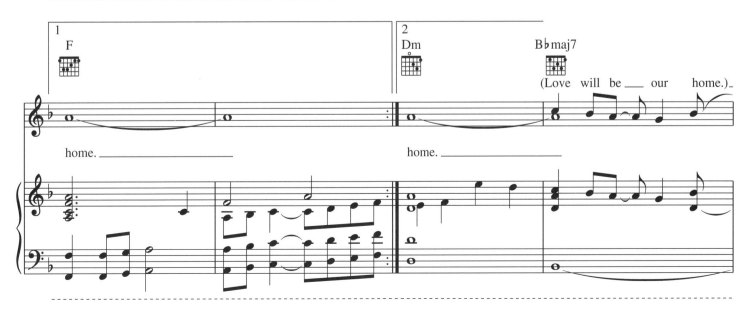

home. ___

(Love will be ___ our home.) ___

home. ___

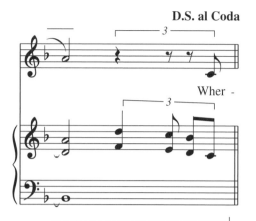

Wher-

Love ___ will,

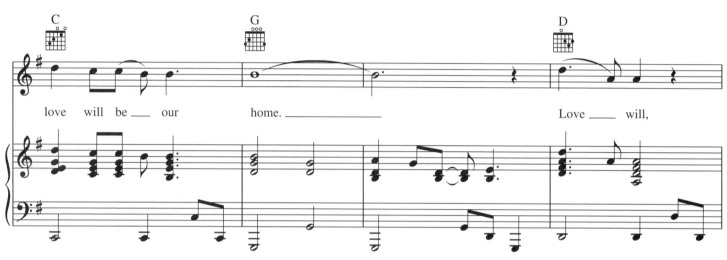

love will be ___ our home. ___ Love ___ will,

love will be ___ our home.

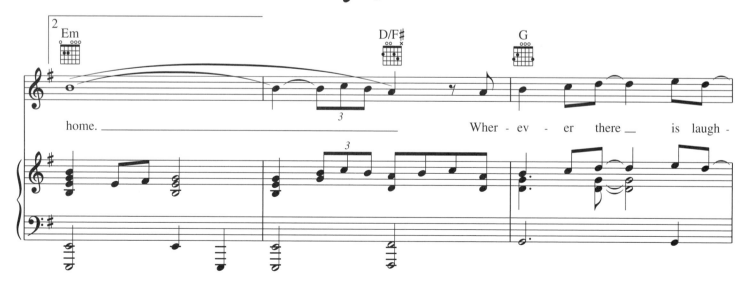

home. ___ Wher-ev-er there ___ is laugh-

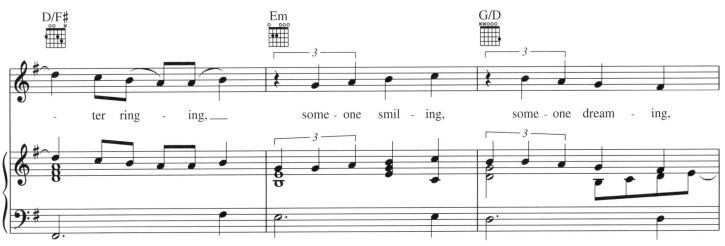

-ter ring - ing,___ some-one smil-ing, some-one dream-ing,

we can live to-geth - er there ___ 'cause love will be ___ our home.

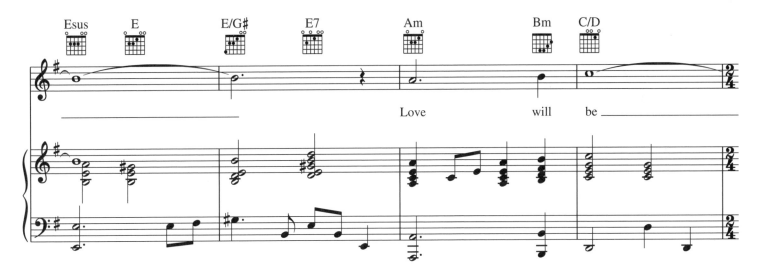

Love will be ___

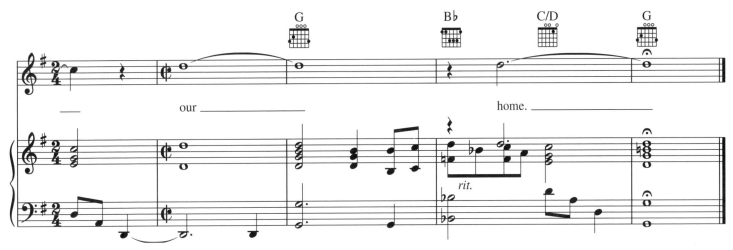

___ our ___ home. ___

rit.

MY PLACE IS WITH YOU

Words and Music by MICHAEL PURYEAR
and GEOFFREY THURMAN

I've walked a - long a hun - dred high - ways,
I've had my prom - is - es for - sak - en

some I wish I could for - get.
in too man - y emp - ty words.

And I've burned a lot of bridg - es
And I'm a - mazed and so a - stound - ed

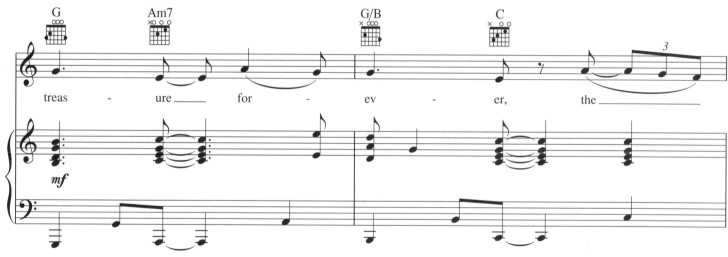

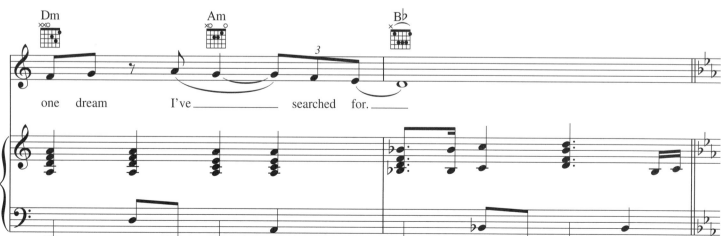

I've not been giv-en my_____

_____ to-mor-rows,_____ I'm on-ly cer-tain of___ to-day.___

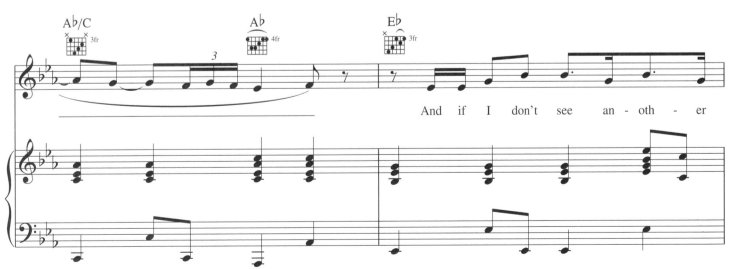

And if I don't see an-oth-er

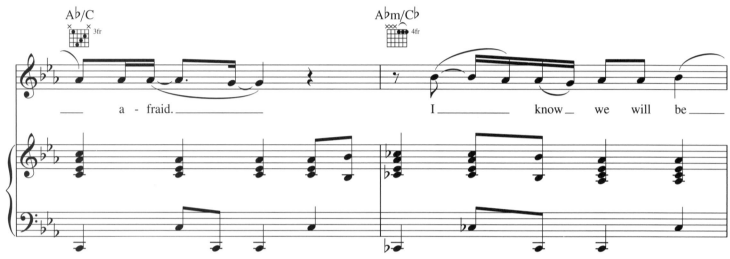

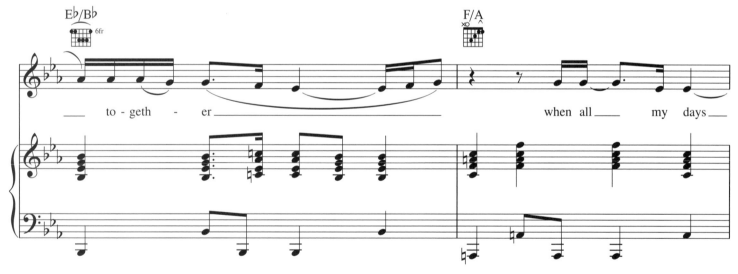

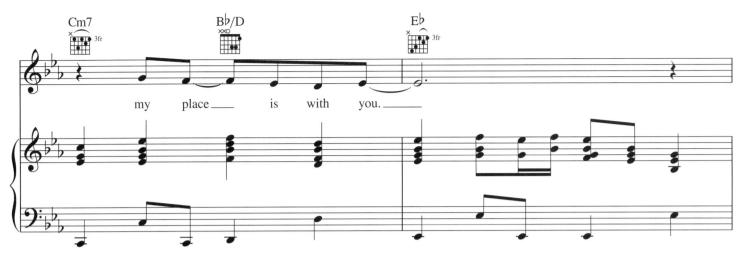

my place ___ is with you. ___

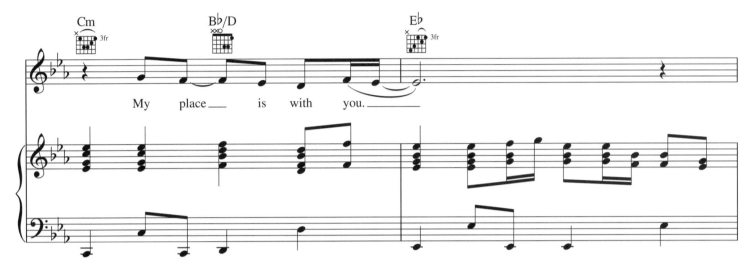

My place ___ is with you. ___

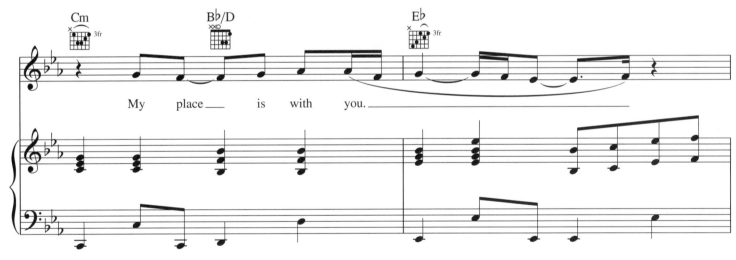

My place ___ is with you. ___

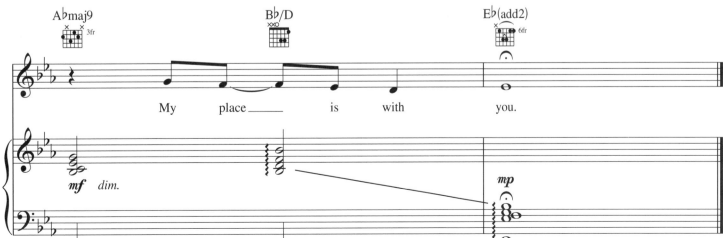

My place ___ is with you.

ODE TO JOY
from SYMPHONY NO. 9 IN D MINOR

By LUDWIG VAN BEETHOVEN

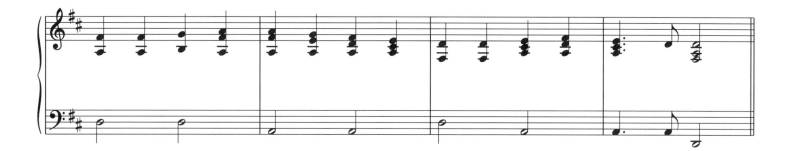

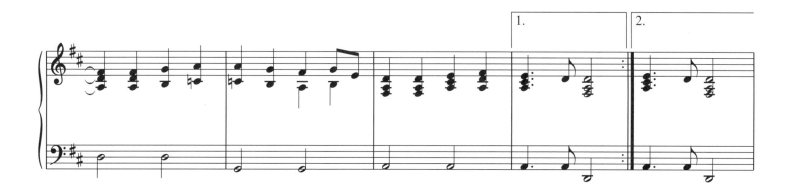

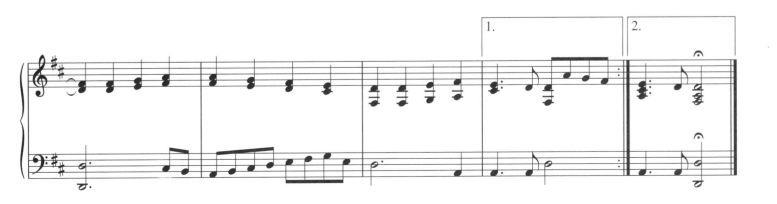

PANIS ANGELICUS
(O Lord Most Holy)

By CÉSAR FRANCK

Poco lento

Pa - nis an -

ge - li - cus   fit   pa - nis   ho - mi - num,   Dat   pan - is

coe - li - cus fi - gu - ris ter - mi - num.   O   res mi -

ra - bi - lis man - du - cat Do - mi - num,   Pau - per,

pau - per,   ser - vus et hu - mi - lis,   Pau - per,

pau - per,   ser - vus et hu - mi - lis.

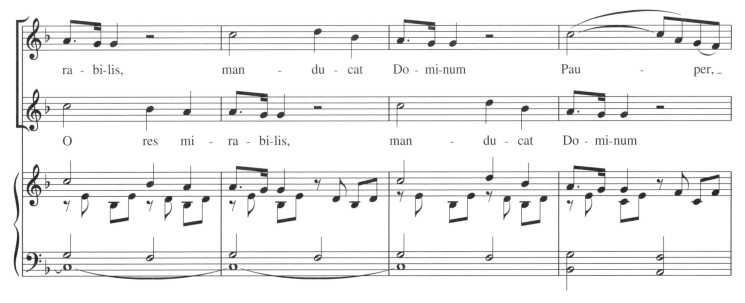

ra - bi-lis, man - du - cat Do - mi-num Pau - per, _

O res mi - ra - bi-lis, man - du - cat Do - mi-num

pau - per, ser - vus et hu - mi - lis, Pau - per, _

Pau - per, _ ser - vus et hu - mi - lis, Pau - per, _

I,II unison

pau - per, ser - vus, _ ser - vus et hu - mi - lis.

SEEKERS OF YOUR HEART

Words and Music by MELODIE TUNNEY,
DICK TUNNEY and BEVERLY DARNALL

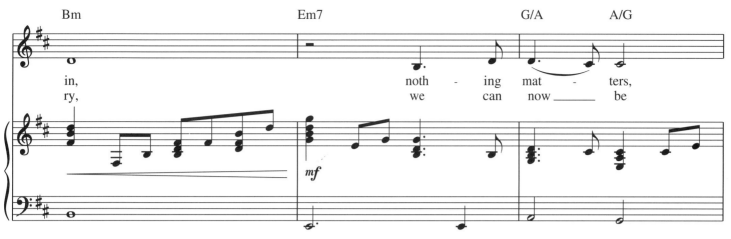

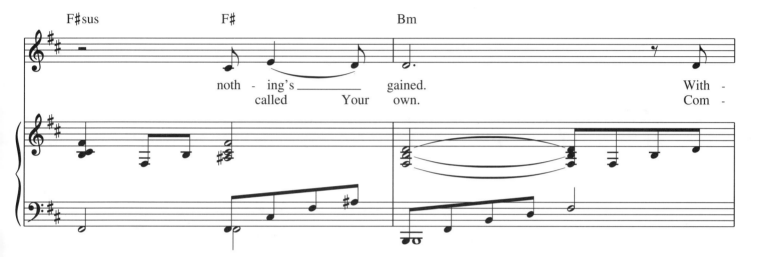

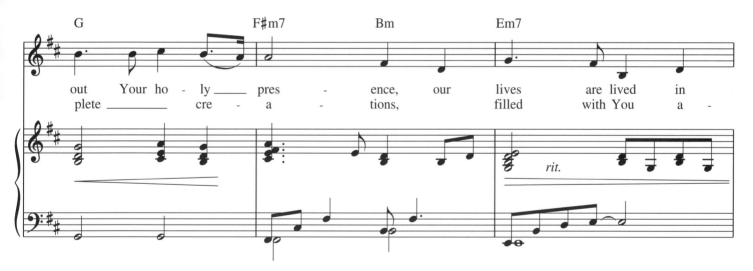

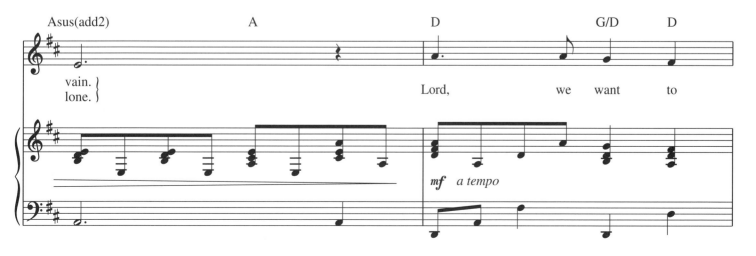

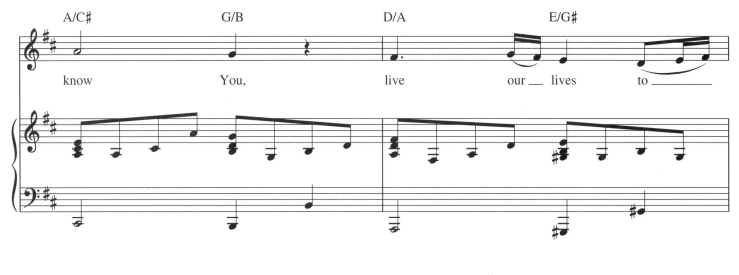

know You, live our ___ lives to ___

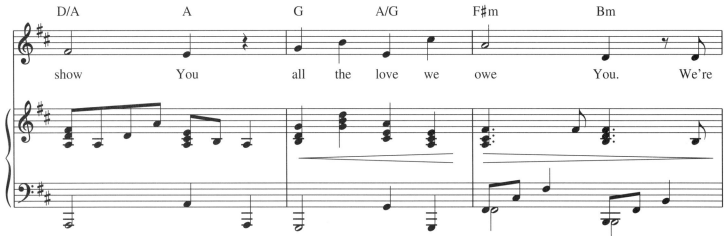

show You all the love we owe You. We're

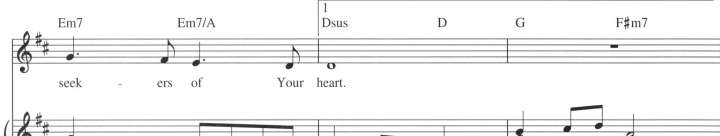

seek - ers of Your heart.

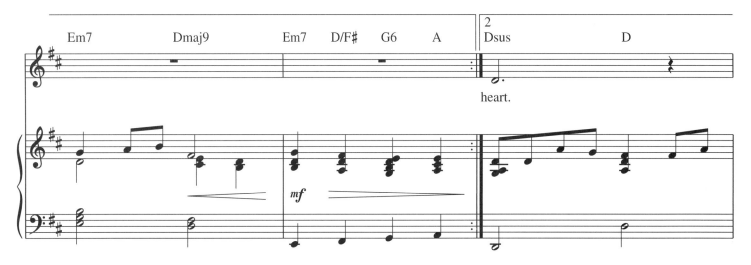

heart.

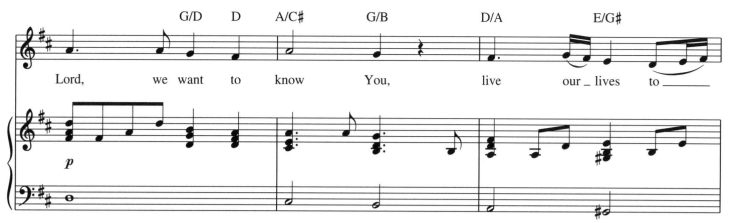

Lord, we want to know You, live our lives to ____

show You all the love we owe You. We're

seek - ers of Your heart. ____

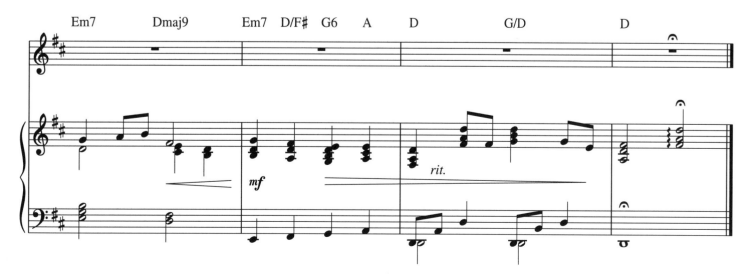

SHEEP MAY SAFELY GRAZE

By JOHANN SEBASTIAN BACH

Andante

SHINE ON US

Words and Music by MICHAEL W. SMITH
and DEBBIE SMITH

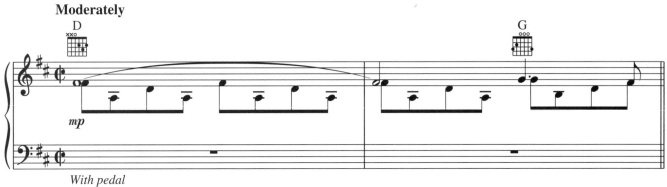

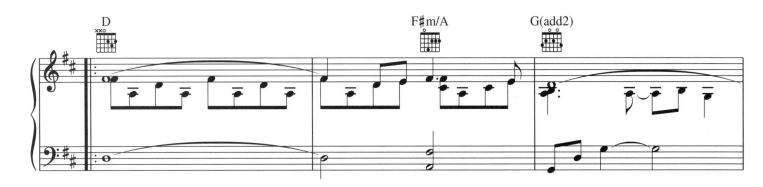

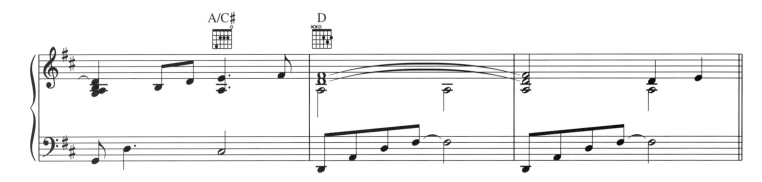

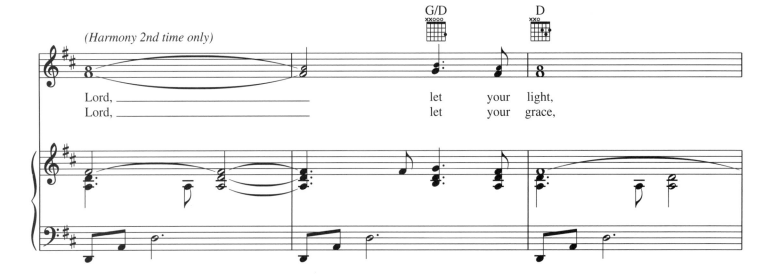

(Harmony 2nd time only)

Lord, _____ let your light,
Lord, _____ let your grace,

STANDING IN THE SON

Words and Music by PETER YORK
and RICHARD SOUTHER

Man is some-times called to live a-lone,
wom-en dream of hav-in' one to care for,

but lone-li-ness is hard for one to car -
for car-ing is a word they un-der-stand.

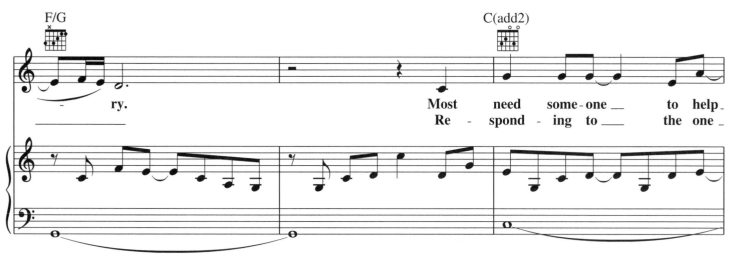

F/G   C(add2)

- ry.

Most need some-one __ to help __
Re - spond - ing to __ the one __

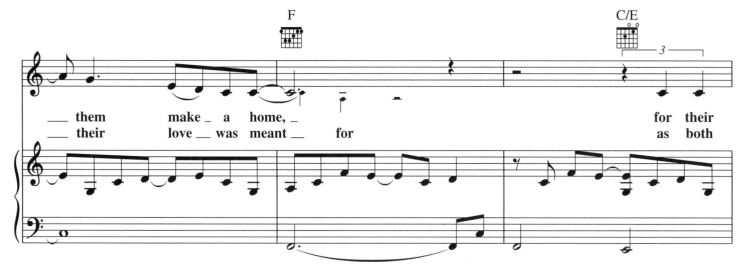

F   C/E

__ them make __ a home, __   for their
__ their love __ was meant __ for   as both

Dm7   F/G   Csus2

love won't be __ com - plete   un - til __ they mar - ry. __
hearts are fash - ioned by   their Mas - ter's hand. __

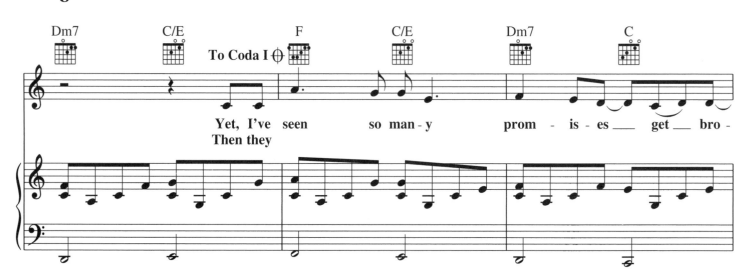

Dm7   C/E   F   C/E   Dm7   C

To Coda I ⊕

Yet, I've seen so man - y prom - is - es __ get __ bro -
Then they

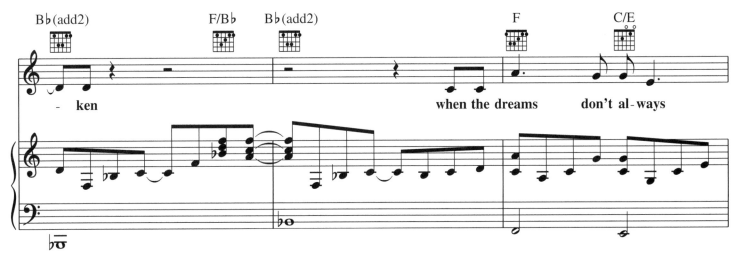

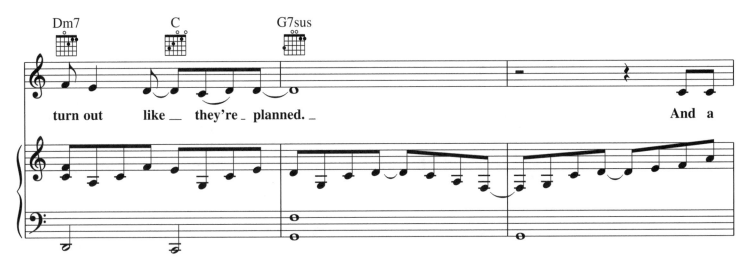

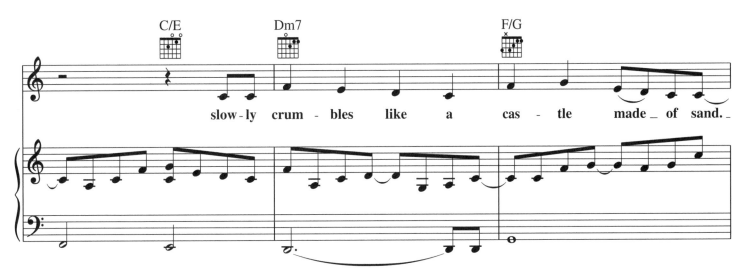

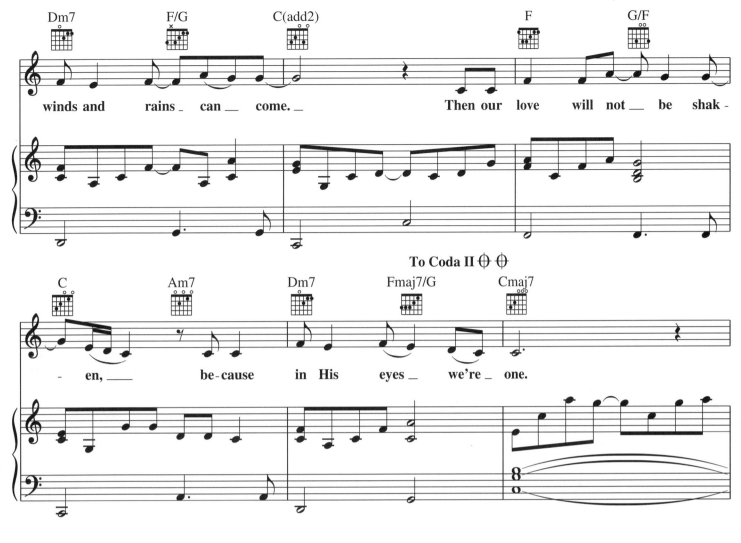

winds and rains _ can _ come. _ Then our love will not _ be shak -

To Coda II ⊕ ⊕

- en, ___ be-cause in His eyes _ we're _ one.

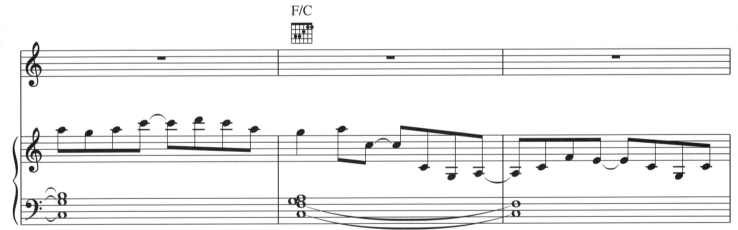

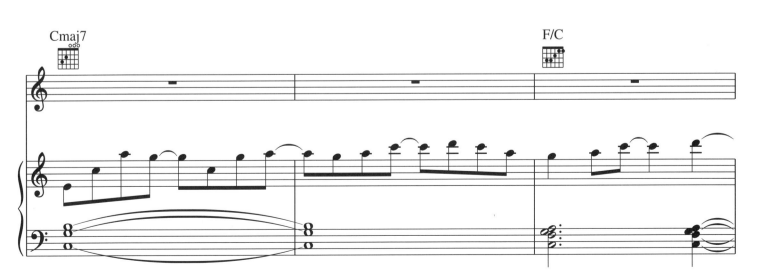

D.S. al Coda I

Some

CODA I

walk this life _____ to-geth-

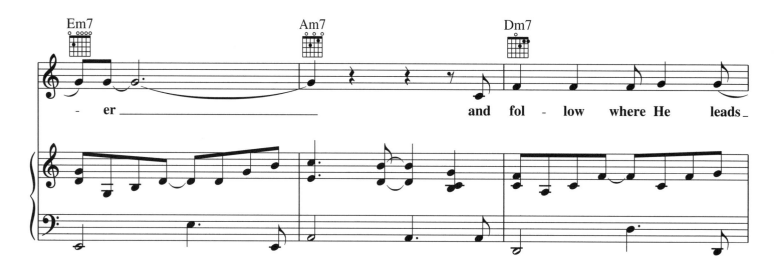

-er _____ and fol - low where He leads_

_____ them hand in hands. _____ And

as they reach _____ the sum-mit of ___ their _____

years, they'll look back to the day _____ it all ___ be-gan. ___

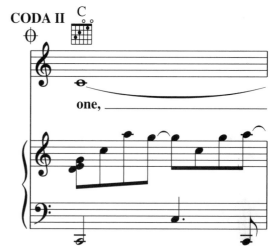

D.S.S. al Coda II

CODA II

So let's

one, ___

stand - in' __ in the Son. _____

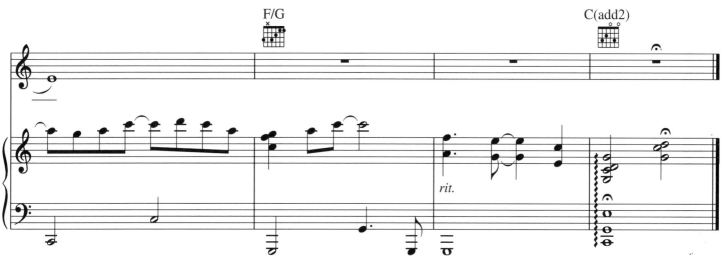

THIS FLAME

Words and Music by MARGARET BECKER,
RICK ELIAS and LINDA ELIAS

Moderately slow

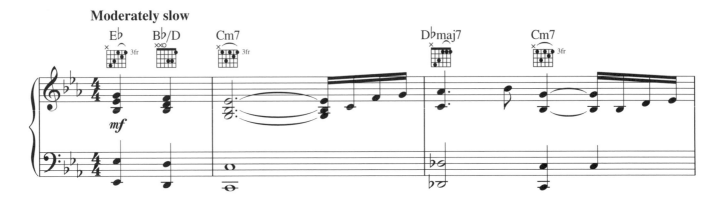

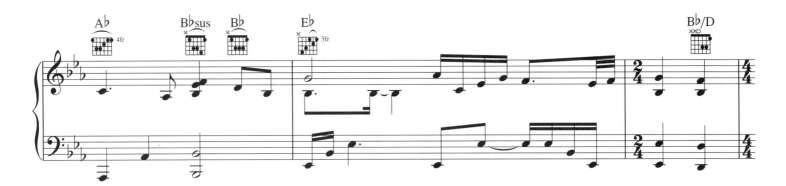

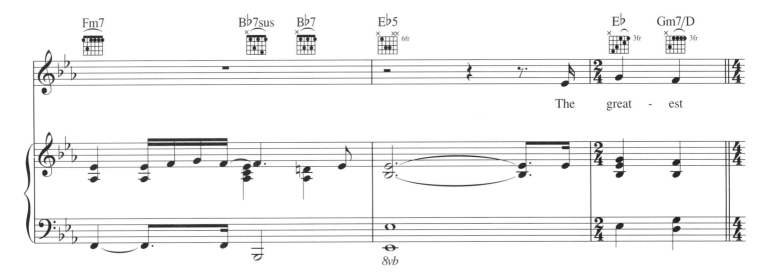

The great - est

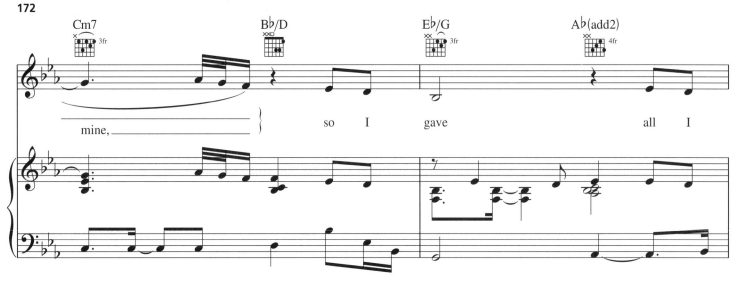

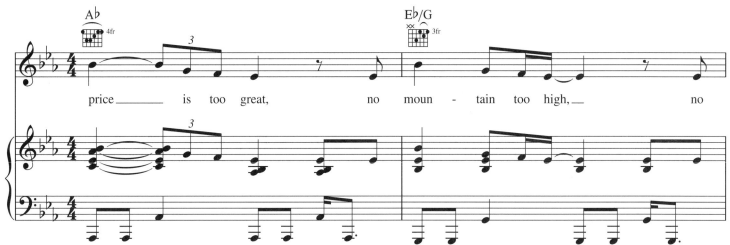

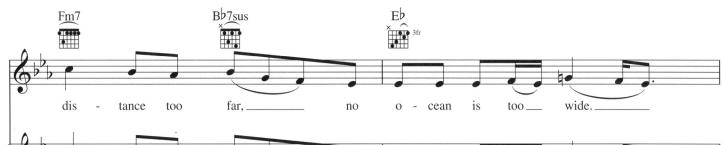

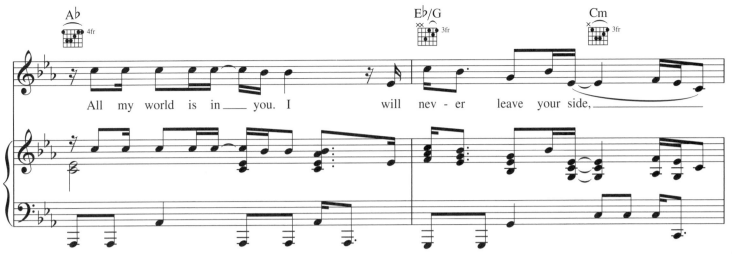

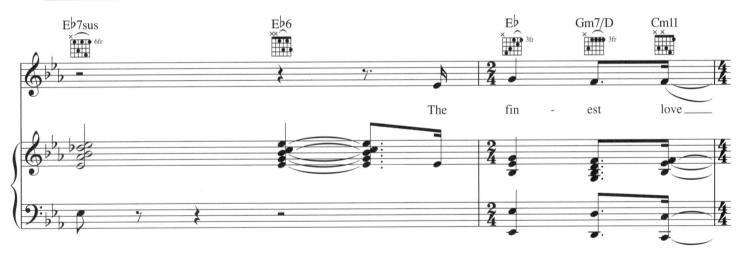

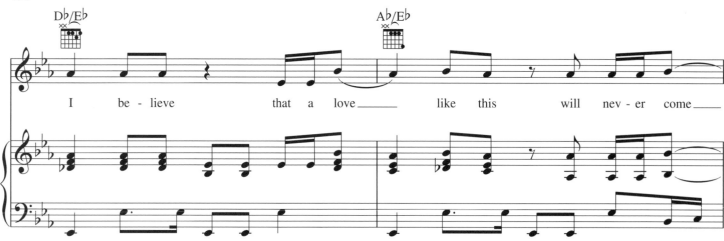

I be-lieve that a love _____ like this will nev-er come _____

_____ to an end, ___ no. Whoa, _____

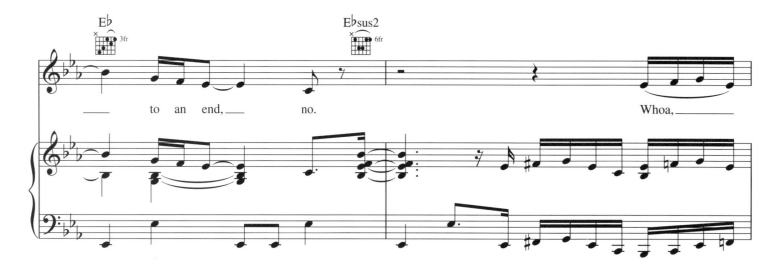

all I have and all _____ my life, I'd give it all _____

Slower

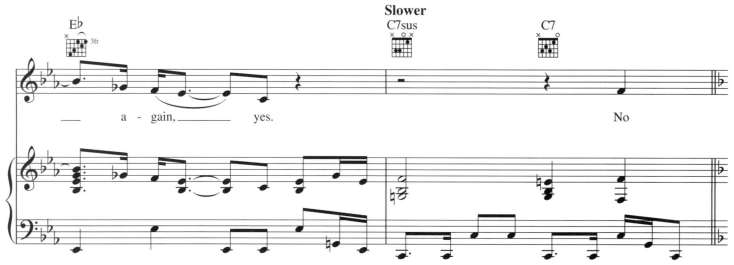

_____ a-gain, _____ yes. No

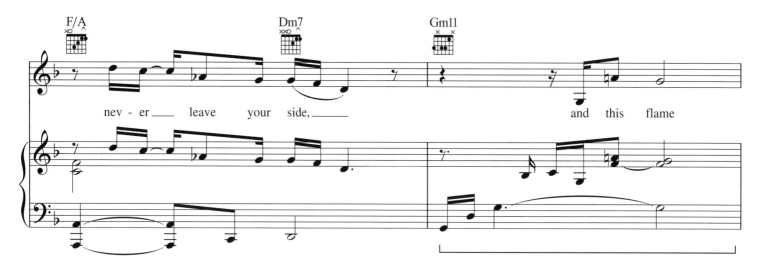

TO KEEP LOVE ALIVE

Words and Music by SCOTT DENTÉ,
CHRISTINE DENTÉ and CHARLIE PEACOCK

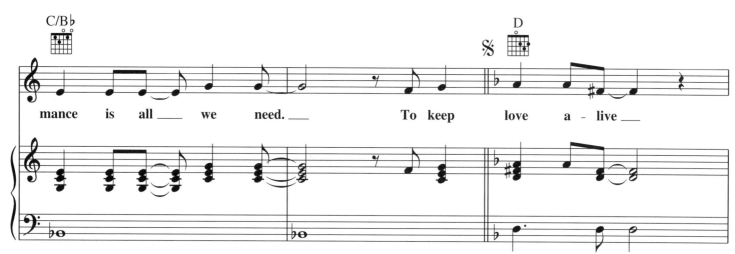

We won't __ live a lie __ and say __ it will __ be eas-

-y __ to __ keep love __ a - live. __

I can't __ i - mag-

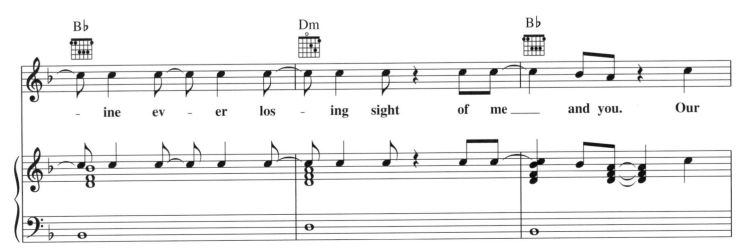

-ine ev - er los - ing sight of me __ and you. Our

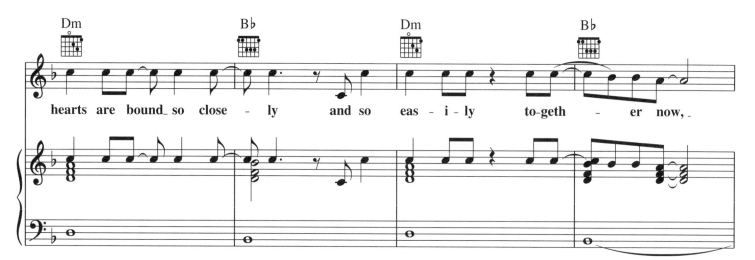

hearts are bound so close - ly and so eas - i - ly to-geth - er now, __

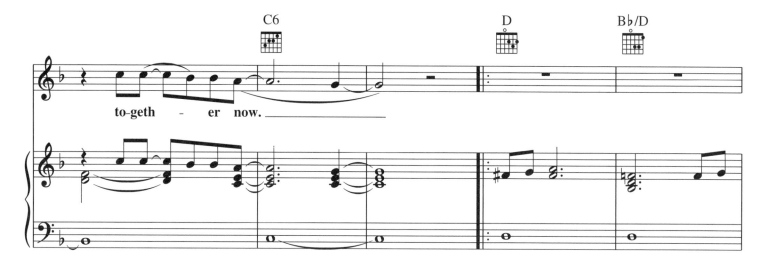

to-geth - er now. _____

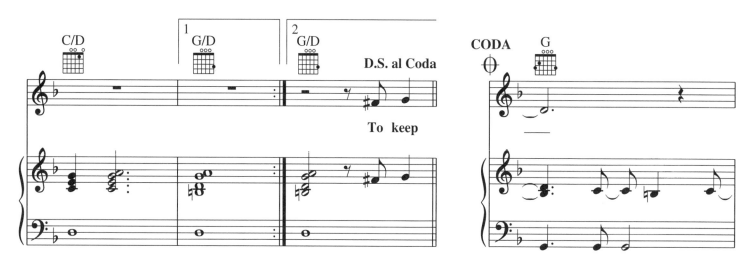

To keep

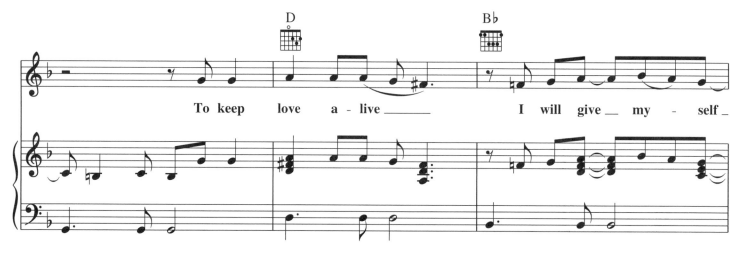

To keep love a - live _____ I will give __ my - self _

un - self - ish - ly ___ when hard times ___ come,

___ they're sure _ to come ___ some - day. ___ We won't _

___ live a lie _ and say ___ it will _ be eas - y ___ to _

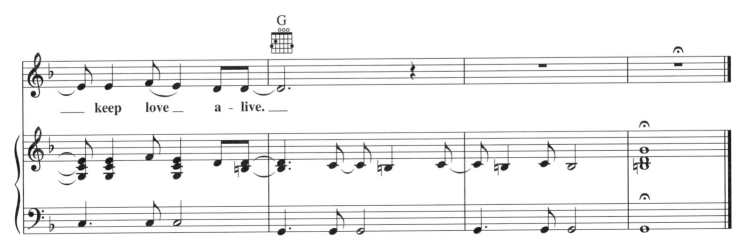

___ keep love _ a - live. ___

'TIL THE END OF TIME

Words and Music by
STEVE GREEN

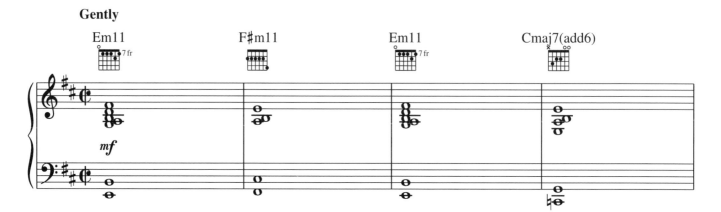

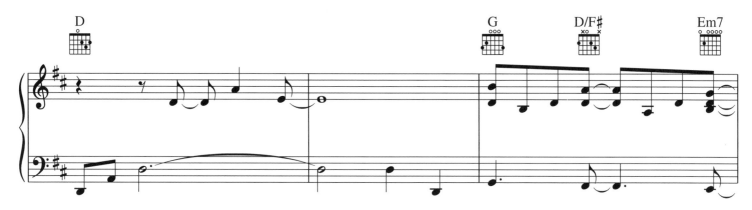

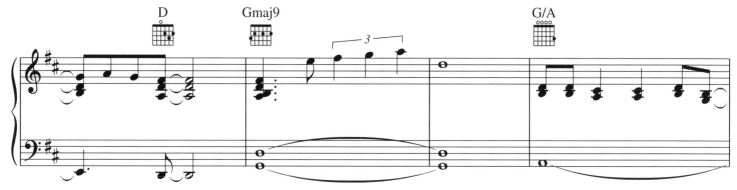

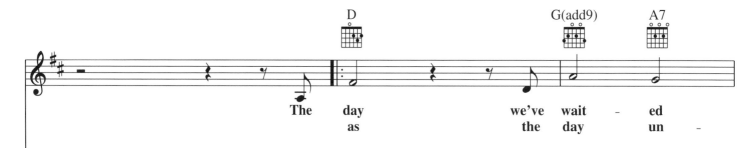

The day   we've wait - ed
as   the   day   un -

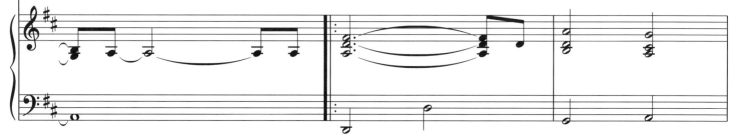

veil   your   heart, __   the   prom-ise   that __   I   make. __
dark-est   night, __   His   prom-ise   calms __   our   fears. __

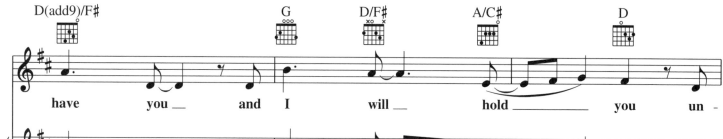

I   will __

have   you __   and   I   will __   hold __   you   un-

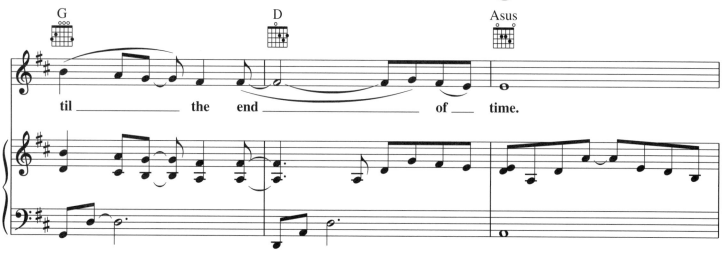

til __   the   end __   of __   time.

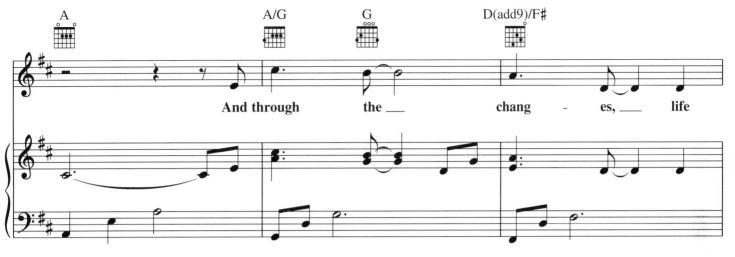

And through the ___ chang - es, ___ life

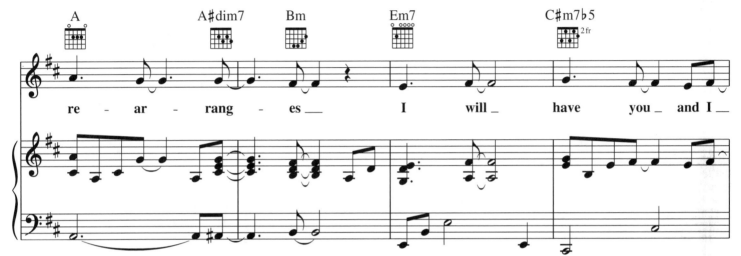

re - ar - rang - es ___ I will ___ have you ___ and I ___

___ will ___ hold _____ you un - til _____ the end ___

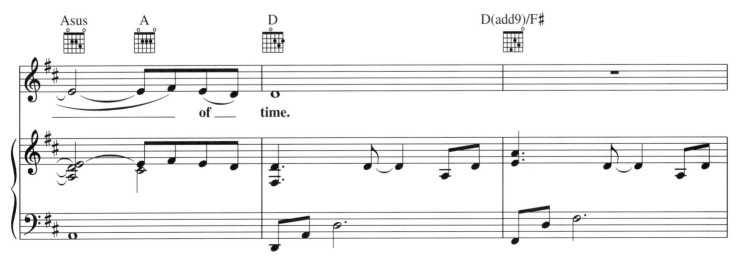

_____ of ___ time.

un - til _____ the end _____

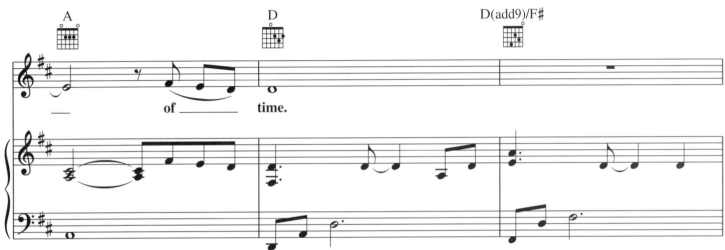

of _____ time.

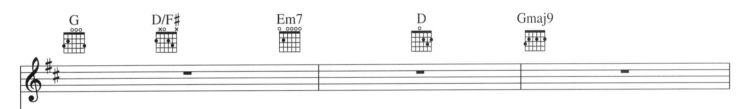

THE WEDDING

Words and Music by
MICHAEL CARD

Lord ___ of light, oh come to this wed-ding; ___ take ___ the doubt and

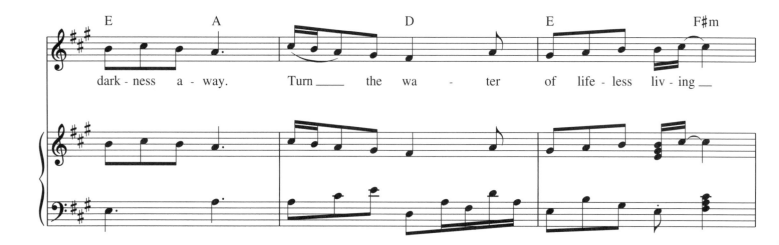

dark-ness a-way. Turn ___ the wa - ter of life-less liv-ing ___

come to this wed - ding; _ take _____ the doubt and dark - ness a - way.

Turn _____ the wa - ter of life - less liv - ing _ to the _ wine _____ of _

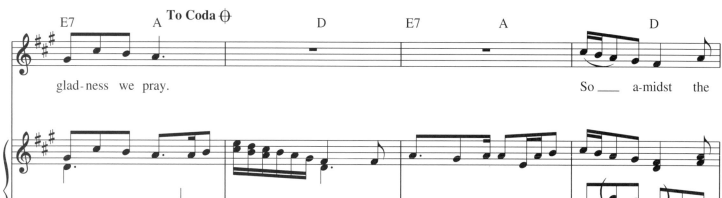

To Coda

glad - ness we pray. So _____ a - midst the

laugh - ter and feast - ing there _____ sits Je - sus full with the fun. He has

made____ them wine be - cause He is long-ing for a ____ wed - ding

D.S. al Coda   **CODA**

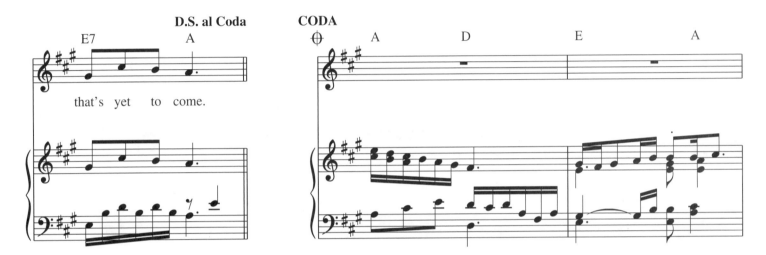

that's yet to come.

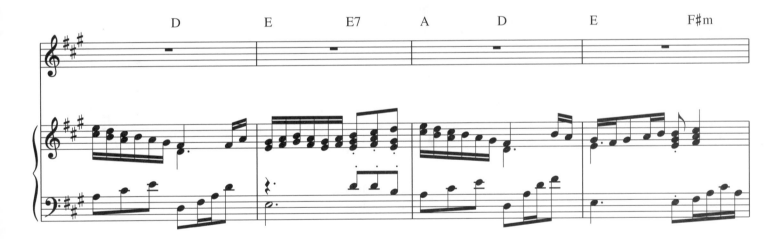

rit.

WHERE THERE IS LOVE

Words and Music by PHILL McHUGH
and GREG NELSON

Where there is love the bruised can find a ref-uge to be held close un-til their tears are gone. Where there is

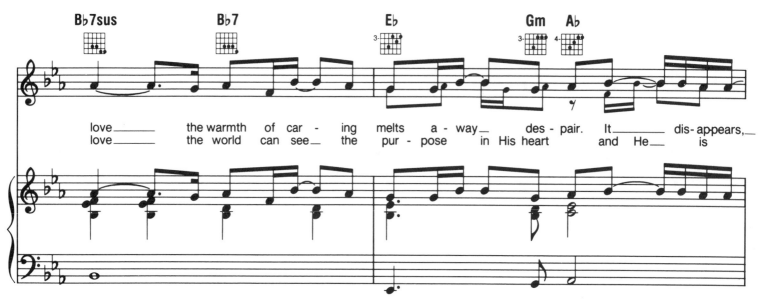

love_____ the warmth of car - ing melts a - way__ des - pair. It_____ dis- ap-pears,
love_____ the world can see__ the pur - pose in His heart and He__ is

_____ known, it_____ dis - ap - pears,_____ Where there is
known, Yes,__ He is known.

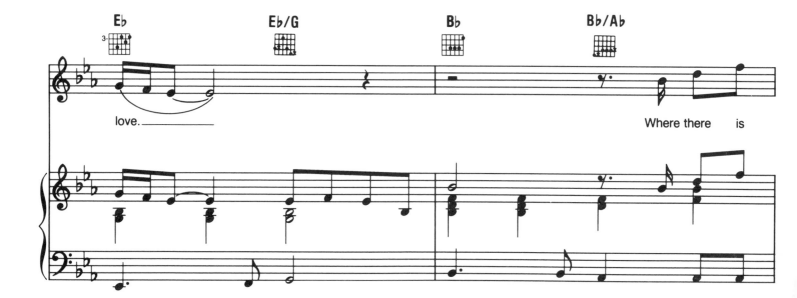

love._____ Where there is

WEDDING PRAYER

Words and Music by
MARY RICE HOPKINS

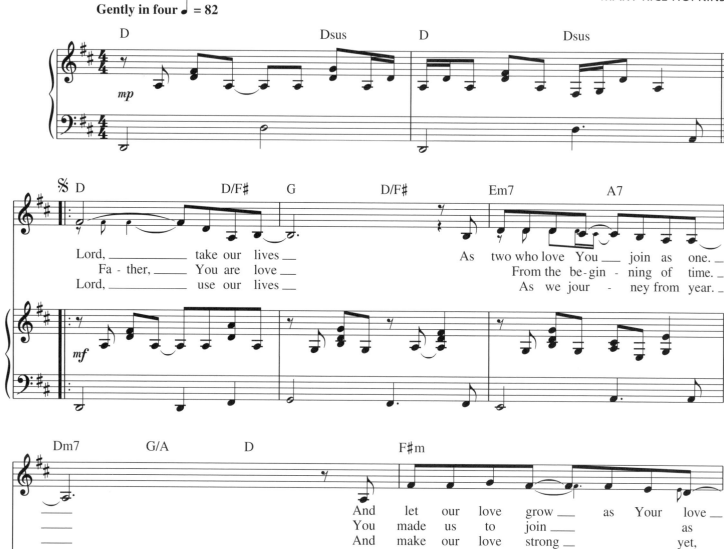

blessed our ___ lives, ___ And You saved us in - side, ___ Now, to -

D.S. al Coda

geth - er we want _ to serve You. _____ So,

CODA

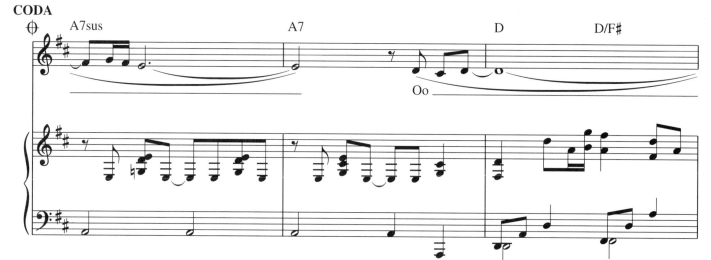

Oo _____

_ Oo Oo _____ Oo.